A Method of
Lighting the Stage

Fourth Edition
Amended and Revised

STANLEY McCANDLESS

THEATRE ARTS BOOKS

NEW YORK

Fourth Edition
Amended and Revised

Copyright, 1932, by Stanley McCandless
Copyright, 1939, by Stanley McCandless
Copyright, 1947, by Stanley McCandless
© 1958, by Stanley McCandless

Fourth Edition, 1958

Corrected Reprint, 1963
Seventh Printing, 1984

The author wishes to acknowledge the invaluable
assistance rendered by Mrs. Edith J. R. Isaacs
in the preparation of the first edition of this book
and by his colleagues and publisher in the succeed-
ing editions.

LIBRARY OF CONGRESS CATALOG CARD NUMBER: 58-10331

ISBN 0-87830-082-1

PRINTED IN THE UNITED STATES OF AMERICA

Contents

ILLUSTRATIONS

FOREWORD TO THE FOURTH EDITION

MUCH HAS happened in the field of stage lighting since this little book first made its appearance. The ellipsoidal reflector spotlight had not been developed; the fresnel spot was just appearing in 1932. The electronic dimmer had only been thought of, and even the autotransformer was scarcely considered as useful in the theatre. Most of these important developments in the field of equipment and more have become integrated into our basic layouts for lighting the stage. In many respects the objectives of the system laid out here can now be more easily achieved. Also along with the great physical improvements—release from artistic as well as technical limitations—the principles of the "method" still serve as a valid technique for lighting most dramatic productions.

There is some justification for the criticism that there is no specific chapter on control—switchboards. There should be a separate book on the subject for the student. So much has happened in this field since the war that a book written a year or so ago would already be obsolete in most technical details. The "method" does imply the objectives of control—the regulation of intensity, color, distribution and movement — over various groups of lights and even indicates the number of circuits for separate dimmer control. But this vitally important and rapidly developing aspect of stage lighting needs to be explained in an organized and simplified way to the student or beginner in the theatre probably in a separate book.

There are also questions as to how the "method" applies to "Arena" type of production. Less often the problems of lighting musical shows, pageants, ballets, and even circuses come up. The answer is not precise, but the basic principles of the "method" really hold.

Just as it is necessary to treat the "method" with great latitude—by using some times more specials than standard acting area units—so should each problem of lighting be approached to give the most direct expression to dramatic visual effect. Visibility, naturalism, composition, and atmosphere are the objectives for lighting no matter what the form of theatre or type of production.

INTRODUCTION

STAGE LIGHTING excites the interest of almost every theatre goer because of its basic dramatic character. It gives visibility where and when it is wanted. It simulates the wonders of natural light; the glory of a colorful sunset, the coziness of the campfire. It expands the horizon of the artist to bring life to color even beyond the vividness of the stained glass window and it vitalizes a plastic picture with lights and darks, deep shadows and glaring highlights if desired, as no other visual medium of design can provide. And finally in its brightness and darkness, its color and pattern, it creates an atmosphere that is inherently dramatic; maybe not always what we expect but a challenge to conquer and to control the medium *light* which is a sense provides a new horizon for artistic expression.

Stage lighting can also lead the way in other uses of light. With a free choice such as the stage gives us, the limitations of cost and practicality are non-existent to a large degree and flexibility and adjustment are provided to allow the imagination of the artist free reign. It is to this new artistic endeavor that this book is dedicated. And it is within the discipline of the theatre in its best sense that dramatic lighting will flourish.

The design, or more specifically, the planning and

execution of the lighting for a production is often surrounded by a veil of mystery which is due, undoubtedly, to lack of knowledge of both the limits and the potentialities of the problem. This mystery arises first from the fundamental lack of philosophy of precedent in the use of light as a design medium, second, from the primitive equipment employed, and third, from the absence of a simple, well defined plan which may be applied to the solution of lighting problems. Here is a plan by which most productions can be lighted.

The chief reason for developing such a plan is to give the young designer or technician the confidence with which to face the real problems of lighting. The art of lighting is not measured by ingenuity, although the complicated technical nature of the subject often leads people to applaud an exhibition of technical mastery, which in terms of the other visual arts might be considered merely a mechanical trick.

This plan prepares the palette, as it were, of the lighting designer, and suggests a practical method of using the tools that are available, but it does not pretend to guarantee the final results of balance and composition in dramatic pictures. The final result depends upon the eye and taste of the designer. Moreover the method does not solve all the problems of lighting; it is in fact simply an effort to clear the ground for actual expression and experimentation. Following it saves a great deal of time, energy and expense; and it has stood the practical test of varied types of production practice.

From the practical point of view, a definite plan has many advantages:

(1) It can provide a standard layout for figuring the cost of a new installation of lighting equipment and it can also be the basis for future elaboration.

(2) In this respect it may be an aid to an architect or building committee, who are generally unacquainted with the amount and kind of lighting equipment necessary for the theatre. Out of a desire to economize on a building budget, items not recognized as a necessary minimum are the first to be curtailed with the result that the lighting layout is generally restricted to footlights and borders with perhaps one or two dimmers. As a matter of fact, such equipment can at best provide only "worklight" illumination, and there are many stock lighting fixtures which cost half the price and give even better results. Such a limited layout is actually a waste of money and it permits little more than lecture or concert platform illumination.

(3) The plan outlines in advance the essential features of good switchboard design, and indicates by the number and wattage of separately regulated units, the number of circuits and controls recommended for the switchboard. This feature is important since the ability to use light dramatically is limited enough, even with the best modern equipment, without sacrificing flexibility of control. Two or three dimmers with noisy snap switches

are as primitive as a one-cylinder motor in an automobile.

(4) Finally, the plan encourages the technician, designer and producer to use light in all its qualities within the practical limits established by the instruments.

A great hope of the modern theatre lies in the development of amateur production. Lighting, as an essential part of dramatic expression today, should be encouraged by an understanding of its use and by the provision of a layout which, while not as elaborate as that used in professional productions, is fundamentally modern and sound and at least adequate to permit good lighting. It is a common error to suppose that the enthusiasm and energy of the amateur can overcome technical limitations which are never found in the professional theatre. On the contrary handicaps which are too great usually absorb the spirit to such an extent that the determination to achieve a planned result is killed at the start.

There must be variety in application. No two stages are ever quite the same and productions differ sufficiently to demand a lighting layout in each case. It will be found that considerable flexibility is provided by using special instruments to cover particular areas or objects, by reducing or increasing the number of standard acting areas, and by varying the intensity, color and distribution obtainable with the standard layout within the separately lighted areas. Experience has demonstrated that this plan includes the least equipment that has any pretense to flexibility. Further elaboration in the number of instruments and special equipment often simplifies the setting up and operation during the performance, but does not materially increase the flexibility.

The pictorial aspect of the stage depends upon the form and color of the setting, the arrangement of the properties, and the grouping and costumes of the actors. These are basic elements that present definite conditions to be blended together, by the distribution of light, into an appropriate dramatic picture or series of pictures. To achieve this there must, first, be light for visibility. There was a time when this was all that lighting contributed to the stage. In those days of brilliant footlights and many rows of open trough borders, a general distribution was all that could be expected; backdrops bore large vistas and monumental architecture which waved majestically in every back stage draught. Everything on the stage appeared flat and of equal importance. The invention of the electric lamp has provided high-powered individual sources that can be controlled from a centralized point, the switchboard. Controlled light is more than a medium to promote or limit visibility. It affects the appearance of all the elements of the stage and by this power becomes a determining element in the composition of a stage picture.

Poor, careless, inadequate and inartistic lighting, of

which there is still a great deal, cannot all be blamed on inexpert handling of lighting equipment. The average theatre is designed with little consideration for the lighting of the stage. Moreover, the standard specifications of many equipment companies are misleading in that they naturally tend to encourage the installation of a type of equipment which is usually antiquated and easy to make, satisfactory for the demands of musicals and concert platforms, but not primarily suited to the needs of the legitimate stage. The layout here suggests the standard minimum quantity of each type of instrument for the uses of the legitimate theatre.

Since the primary function of lighting is to give controlled visibility this influences all its other functions. Perhaps some day more efficient and more powerful instruments will enable us to approach the distribution and visibility given by daylight and the sun. It may also be possible to reduce the number of instruments to advantage. But it must be borne in mind that it is not a factual presentation that is desirable on the stage, it is the representation of some effect that contains the essence of reality. If it were possible to place an actual scene on the stage, sunlight and all, it would probably not be any more dramatic than a photograph. On the stage the visibility of the actor is an arbitrary fundamental. If, at the same time, he can be surrounded by a special atmosphere that is convincingly dramatic, it makes no difference whether the light comes from one source or several, so long as the effect is not distracting.

Any arbitrary method will, of course, have its objections as well as its advantages. A valid objection to the fixed layout presented here is its inflexible nature; another is the necessity of using a particular instrument in the same place for all situations. But, while the plan should not be interpreted so narrowly as to exclude the selection of a special instrument to perform a specific duty, there must always be a compromise between the selection of a particular group of instruments, colors and accessories in definite positions (a set-up) for each scene, and a simple layout for all the scenes of the whole performance. Although the set-up suggested here is more or less the same for all productions, it is quite possible that under special conditions only special instruments carefully chosen to perform specific duties may be used to light a scene.

The instruments incorporated in the normal layout should generally be of the portable type so that they may be mounted in a number of different positions to conform to the special conditions established by any production. They should be mounted so that they are accessible for renewing lamps when they burn out or even for changing direction and colors between scenes if desired. And there should be a sufficient number of current outlets reaching these positions to allow for the individual control of each instrument, and color circuit.

A discussion of lighting instruments and the methods

of their use would be incomplete without some mention of the objects and surfaces that lighting makes visible to the audience. Scenery, costumes and even makeup can be called secondary lighting instruments because light is really not visible until it strikes some surface so that it can be reflected to the eye. But such a discussion comes primarily under the heading of scenic design and its relation to light. This book tries only to indicate how far scenery is the determining factor in achieving a result and how its design influences the use of light and equipment.

A layout such as this is no more foolproof than the average automobile; but with a little experience and care, anyone can use the equipment effectively just as readily as he can learn to drive. Too often in theatres the untrained and careless are thrust into positions that demand skill and knowledge, and it is hardly fair to limit the technical possibilities of production by such methods. The ingenious and artistic person may achieve good results with even less equipment than is indicated here. Lighting a production is, however, not an individual expression, but rather a co-ordinate part of the whole, and there is little chance that the method of expression of the playwright, actor, producer and designer will conform to any greater simplification than this.

PROCEDURE

THE fundamental lighting of a production is outlined by the playwright's manuscript. The indications of place and the time of day, demanding specific details such as lamp-light, sunlight, moonlight, etc. (which are called motivating sources), are unconsciously or consciously dictated by the playwright. The producer may adhere to these details or change them. He gives the designer and technician the necessary information with which to set to work, and the lighting plan is then further determined by the setting and the structural characteristics of the stage. Unfortunately up to this point in the procedure, the problems and limitations of lighting are usually very little considered. Each playwright and producer considers lighting in terms of what he has seen in the past, or what he would like it to be, to satisfy his own expression. This attitude tends either to conventionalize stage lighting, or to present problems which are impossible to solve. The result is invariably a compromise.

The floor plan of the setting, including the arrangement of the furniture, the position of the walls, openings, background, platforms, etc., establish the possible acting areas. These areas should be specially lighted to give emphasis and visibility to the actor. Theoretically the whole acting area might be lighted with one power-ful instrument directing its beams to the stage from a distance, at an angle which would light up the face of the actor somewhat as the rays from the sun make objects visible on a sunny day.

But we have neither such an instrument nor the physi-cal position from which it can direct its rays to the rather restricted acting area within the setting. It is more prac-tical to use several soft-edge spots in available posi-tions. By dividing the general acting area into a number of sections (generally six), the normal spread of light from each instrument can be expected to cover the actor in each of these sections or acting areas. Under such con-ditions the director can be sure that visibility will be provided for the actor in every available acting area and that there is additional flexibility for heightening some areas and suppressing others—obviously difficult where a single high-powered instrument is used to light the whole acting area.

Having satisfied the director that it is possible to obtain degrees of *visibility* over different parts of the entire acting area so that he is not limited in working out the business of movement (except for the sake of using the motivating light and thereby suppressing the arbitrary nature of the acting area lighting), the de-signer or technician can consider creating a definite effect of time of day and locality, or the opposite—an indefinite time and place. Another set of instruments must be used to create the motivating light (a degree of *naturalism*) and still another to provide the light distribution on the scenery which gives the proper *compositional* quality to the picture, and creates that intangible dramatic essence called *mood*.

Instruments which give specific distributions of light over different parts of the scenery and acting area must then be selected. Inasmuch as the scenery and the acting areas have a general relation to each other, the mounting position for the various types of instruments used to light each part is more or less determined. In this respect the fixed structural arrangements of the stage and auditorium are usually inflexible. The setting therefore should be so designed, in an arrangement of forms, as to permit suitable mounting positions for the lighting instruments. Allowance should be made for the use of instruments around the stage side of the proscenium. Openings in the setting should be designed with respect to the possible position of floor instruments. The back drop or cyclorama should be arranged to permit the placing of lighting instruments to give the best distribution of light over its surface.

With present equipment it is possible (primarily through intensity variation from the switchboard) to control color tonality and the composition of light distribution over the various parts of the stage. Each group of instruments is selected to give a reasonable range of intensity, color, and distribution. Special instruments must be added to the layout to provide motivating light and to create special effects, so that in addition to the control for the normal set-up, an indefinite flexibility is provided for special lighting. Where there are insufficient control units—dimmers, switches, etc.—the flexibility of lighting is correspondingly limited and the lighting plans of each production should take this limitation into account.

Unless switchboards are carefully designed and equipped with every means to simplify the problem of operation, they are apt to be expensive and clumsy pieces of apparatus which limit the possibility of creating subtle lighting. They serve two purposes: to balance the intensity of each unit or group of units, and to permit subtle changes of lighting during the progress of a performance. Due to its size, the position of the "board" (on the stage) usually is such that the operator cannot see the effects he is producing, and since he works blindly he is reduced to making changes mechanically. It is unwise under such conditions to attempt complicated lighting effects or distributions no matter how well they have been conceived. The plans for lighting a production should in all cases be checked against the available means of control.

If it were possible, in advance of rehearsals, to visualize the fitting together of all the elements of a production, no doubt a great deal of time and expense could be saved trying to make them co-ordinate, but this is relatively impossible. A certain amount of latitude must be left in all the elements that receive expression in the production. The color of the light may be right for the setting and the motivating light and yet be wrong for the costumes. An instrument because of its position may make its rays cast a shadow in the wrong place. The balance of intensity from each source cannot be determined until all the properties, setting, etc., are on the stage. However, a general plan which allows for all variables provides the only sound method for lighting the production.

The ultimate control of light must be centered in the switchboard, and this instrument must be so equipped that it can give a control over changes of color and distribution as well as intensity. The perfect switchboard will be compact and as easily operated as an organ console. It will be located, as is already the case in a few instances, in a place where the operator can see what he is doing just as the organist can hear what he plays. Certainly the number of lighting instruments will have to be limited, and this may mean that new stage conventions will replace the old. Probably by that time this whole method of lighting, conceived to give the best results with equipment and practice as they are today, will be superseded by a simpler and better formula.

LAYOUT FOR A MEDIUM-SIZE STAGE

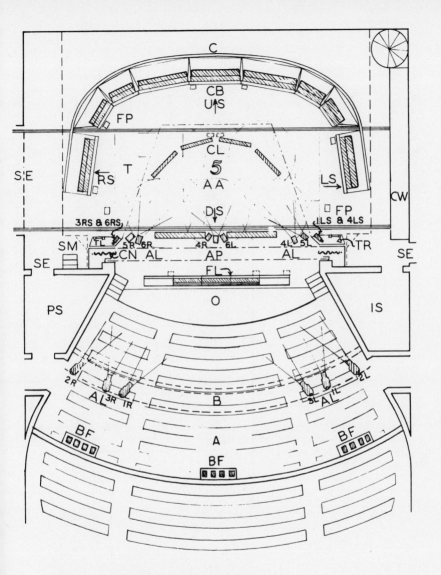

Figure 1: PLAN OF THE STAGE
Position of the instruments, acting areas and various parts of the
stage and auditorium.

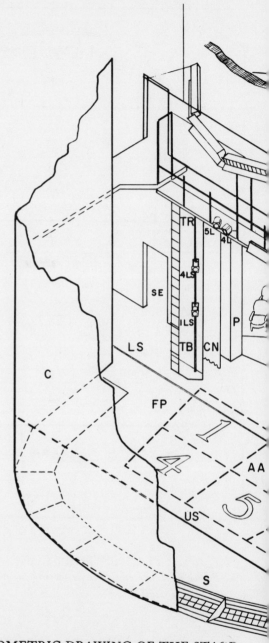

Figure 2: AN ISOMETRIC DRAWING OF THE STAGE
Parts of the proscenium wall and ceiling, and the auditorium are cut away to show positions of instruments and parts of the stage.

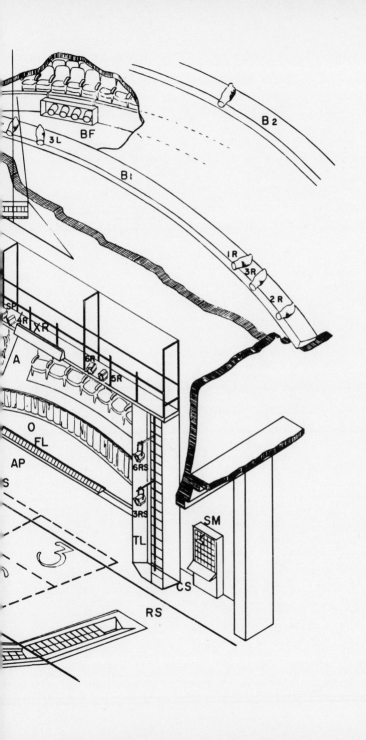

Figure 3: LONGITUDINAL SECTION

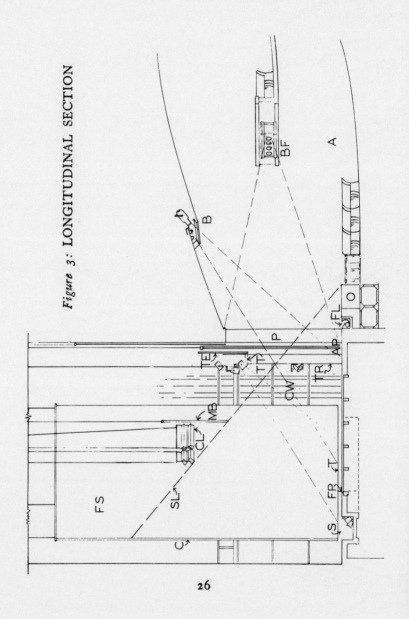

LEGEND

A—Auditorium.

AA—Acting areas.

AL—Acting area lights. The six general positions noted on the plan include the acting area lights numbered according to the area which they cover; *e.g.*, 1ʟ, acting area light from the left; 1ʀ, acting area light from the right. Alternate positions for areas 1ʟ, 4ʟ, 3ʀ, and 6ʀ are indicated behind the tormentor (TR or TL) flipper, mounted on a vertical pipe batten. These alternate positions are useful when space is allowed between the tormentor and the down-stage (DS) end of the set on each side of the stage.

AN—Apron. The front of the stage.

B—Beams. Ceiling coves used to mask the instruments mounted above the ceiling. (See plan and section.)

BF—Balcony front. A box built into or hung on the front of the balcony, used to mask the instruments mounted at this position. Valuable for curtain lighting and most often found in presentation houses. Used to light the curtain and the front acting areas.

C—Cyclorama. A large cloth backdrop hung around three sides of the stage, generally so that it can be raised and lowered.

CL—Cyclorama lights. A bank of high-powered flood lights, or special strips used to illuminate the cyclorama in various colors (Red, Green, and Blue preferred) from the most advantageous position: some distance from the cyclorama. The use of the instruments in this position requires a clear fly space (FS).

CN—Curtain. Act curtain, act drop, or main curtain. Indicated in the "draw" position.

CS—Company switch. Located at stage right. A large capacity switch used to supply current to the portable switchboards usually carried as part of the equipment of travelling companies. In this case, only the house lights, occasionally the footlights (FL) and first border (XR), are controlled by the house switchboard (SW). The portable switchboard is specifically designed for each particular production and is operated by the company electrician or operator who travels with the production.

FL—Footlights. Divided in this plan into five sections and mounted in a pit at the front of the apron (AN). Equipped with a hood to prevent light spilling into the auditorium. (See Chapter III.)

DS—Down-stage. The direction toward the footlights.

FP—Floor pocket. Outlet boxes distributed about the stage (each having 2 to 4 outlets). A small pit sunk in the floor, equipped with a self-closing slotted cover. Floor instruments are connected to the switchboard through these pockets.

FS—Fly space. (See section.) All the space above the acting area to the "grid" into which scenery can be raised for storage or to await its use in a particular scene.

GR—Ground row. A narrow piece of scenery set on the floor at the rear of the stage to represent the distant landscape. It masks the horizon lights (S).

IS—Instrument storage. Storage space for instruments and lighting equipment.

LS—Left stage. A general direction toward the left, determined from the point of view of the actor as he faces the audience.

MB—Masking border. (See section.) A cloth border hung over the stage and used to mask the cyclorama lights (CL), particularly where a high proscenium opening is used.

O—Orchestra pit. A pit sunk in the floor of the auditorium at the front of the stage to accommodate the musicians. This can be covered over as indicated in the section, with a portable platform, and raised to the auditorium floor level for additional seating area, or raised to the stage level to make an extended apron.

P—Proscenium. An open arch framing the stage at the stage side of the auditorium.

PS—Property storage. The room allowed by the slanting walls of the auditorium is often used as property storage or as a quick change dressing room, on account of its close proximity to the stage.

RS—Right stage. General direction to the right, determined from the point of view of the actors as they face the audience.

S—Horizon strips or Cyc foots. Several sections of high-powered concentrating reflector striplights in several colors (generally Red, Green, and Blue, sometimes Amber), either sunk in the floor in the horizon pit, which is equipped with covers, or mounted on movable trucks near the base of a cyclorama.

SE—Stage entrance. Any access to the back-stage space, either for scenery or actors.

SM—Stage manager. Often called the prompt position. The stage manager's desk where cue signals, dressing room signals, curtain signals, a house telephone and the act call bell are located. Always located near to the proscenium, particularly at the point where the act curtain is pulled.

SW—Switchboard. The house switchboard, built in as part of the equipment of the theatre. Generally located on a line with the proscenium, at either side of the stage, either on the stage floor or on a balcony built above it. This switchboard controls the house lights and all the stage lights, and invariably includes dimmers which can vary the intensity of the instruments connected to the outlets distributed about the stage.

T—Traps. The removable sections of the floor of the acting area.

TB—Tormentor batten or boomerang. Vertical pipe batten used for mounting tormentor lights.

TE—Teaser. The overhead masking line of the proscenium.

TL—Tormentor-ladder. Access to tormentor lights and bridge.

TR—Tormentor. The adjustable curtain or wing used on each side of the stage to determine the widths of the proscenium opening.

TT—Teaser thickness. A box teaser, generally used in conjunction with tormentor flipper to make an inner proscenium. Usually adjustable as to height and particularly valuable for masking the teaser instruments—X-Rays (XR) and acting area lights (AL).

US—Up-stage. The general direction toward the rear of the stage.

XR—X-Rays. X-Ray border. Border strips.
1, 2, 3, 4, 5, 6—Sections of the acting area lighted separately.

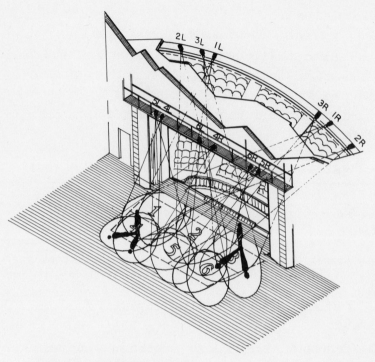

Figure 4: ACTING AREAS

An isometric drawing of the stage viewed from the rear right corner showing the pools of light created by the acting areas. The elliptical pools indicated here as lines are generally soft-edged so that they blend into one another. Thus to the eye there should be no separate pools but apparently an even illumination over the whole acting area. However, the two shadows of the actor are always present and the lights should be so focused that the actor can move in any portion of the numbered areas and be sure that his face and the balance of his body will be lighted. Note that 1L, 3R, 4L *and* 6R *instruments are mounted so that their outside rays are parallel with the side extremities of the whole acting area.*

LIGHTING THE ACTING AREA

THE general acting area is that part of the stage floor which may be used by the actor when he is in view of the audience. For the purpose of lighting it, this area can be assumed to be broken up into smaller sections, six for the average stage, numbered as indicated in *Figure 4*. These smaller areas are contiguous and of more or less the same size and shape. The lighting of these areas is primarily to give adequate and yet variable visibility to the actor's face. The plane of illumination is, therefore, generally considered at this level or about five and one half feet above the stage floor (*Figure 4*).

INTENSITY

The intensity of light illuminating an actor's face is assumed to be adequate for the rest of his body. The amount required for good visibility of the white man or woman actor with the usual make-up varies chiefly according to the amount of contrast between the brightness of the face and the background. Where the background is dark, the illumination of the face can be low. The most important reason for lighting the acting area separately from the background lies in the fact that the average scenery reflects light more brilliantly than the actor's face.

When the acting areas are lighted solely by border

strips and footlights, which give excessive general distribution of light, much more intensity of illumination is required than is necessary with controlled, directed light that is kept off the scenery. Therefore, it is possible to create a greater effect of visibility with less illumination, when contrast is preserved, than under the old system of using footlights and borders exclusively.

The absolute range of illumination necessary for the acting area is difficult to specify and equally difficult to state simply. A normal range may lie between 5 and 50 foot-candles. The foot-candle is technically the amount of illumination given to a surface one foot away from a standard candle, or, roughly, the illumination per watt given by an incandescent lamp. Where a lack of contrast exists, it may be necessary to use 100 to 250 foot-candles, without exaggeration of the object. Since the intensity of illumination varies inversely as the square of the distance from the source, high-powered sources must be used when the instrument is at a distance from the acting area.

Lens units (*Figures 5, 6, 7 and 8*), the instruments used to light the acting area, have the ability to increase the apparent candlepower of the beam of light from a source in a useful direction even though they use relatively little (3% to 25% at most)* of all light created at the source.

---

* *Step lens spotlights (Figures 5B and 9F) having a short focal length lens use from two to four times the number of rays emanating from the source.*

To obtain forty foot-candles of illumination at a distance of twenty feet, an open light source as large as the square of this distance (to offset the drop in intensity due to distance), 20^2 x 40, or 16,000 candle power, must be used. In case a standard spotlight is used the gathering power of the lens itself is so effective that it can condense the rays that would normally emanate from the lamp within a 35-80 degree angle into a beam ranging in spread from 7 to 45 degrees (Figure 9). By means of measuring instruments it has been found that a lamp as small as 750 watts, in a fresnel spotlight, can give a beam powerful enough to supply 55 foot-candles at twenty feet.*

The table in the appendix lists a practical range of intensities for fresnel and ellipsoidal spotlights.

| Plano-convex | | Maximum Candle Power | | | | | |
| Watts | Lens | Beam Spread | | | | | |
		Spot	°	Med.	°	Flood	°
250	5 x 9	10,000	15	2,000	30	1,000	60
400	5 x 9	20,000	15	3,500	30	1,700	60
500	6 x 10	48,000	10	5,000	25	2,500	45
1000	6 x 10	90,000	10	11,000	25	4,500	45
1500	8 x 12	135,000	10	40,000	30	10,000	50
2000	8 x 12	195,000	10	55,000	30	14,000	50

The illumination in foot-candles (f.c.) at a point equals the candle power divided by the square of the distance from the instrument to the point lighted, $f.c. = \dfrac{c.p.}{d^2}$

Example: How much illumination will be given at a distance of 20 feet by a medium beam from a 750 watt fresnel spot?

From above, a 750 watt spot at medium spread (40°) has 22,000 candle power (c.p.). Square 20 feet and divide into 22,000.

$22,000 \div 400 = 55.$ *Illumination will be equal to 55 f.c.*

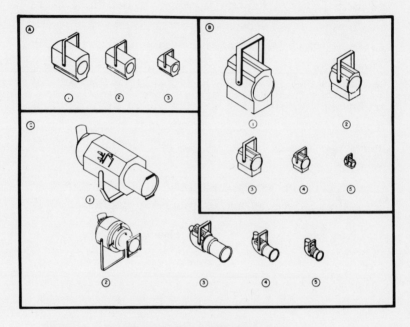

Figure 5: TYPES OF SPOTLIGHTS
An indication of the sizes of 3 different types:
(A) Plano-convex lens spots
 (1) 8″ lens   1000-2000 watts
 (2) 6″ lens   500-1000 watts
 (3) 5″ lens   250- 400 watts

These figures are only approximate and are calculated from the effects given by a certain group of lenses —those normally used with each size of lamp. It is apparent that the focus of the lamp or its position relative to the lens to give a certain spread of light has a considerable influence upon the intensity of the light, and therefore upon the distance at which it can be used effectively (*Figure* 9). As the angle of spread increases the intensity or effective distance decreases, very rapidly at first and more slowly at the wide limit. In fact, the range of distance for each beam spread within the limits which will give from five to fifty foot-candles is so great that the table loses value unless every variable is considered. The 20° spread or medium focus is the beam angle that is most useful in computing the wattage for a certain throw or distance. Another interesting variable lies in the fact that as the intensity decreases rapidly as

---

(B) Fresnel or step-lens spots

   (1) 14 or 16" lens 5000 watts

   (2) 10 or 12" lens 2000 watts

   (3) 8" lens 1000-2000 watts

   (4) 6" lens   250- 750 watts

   (5) 3" lens   100 watts

(C) Ellipsoidal reflector spots

   (1) 12"   lens 3000-5000 watts 10-12° beam

   (2) 8"   lens 1000-2000 watts 20-24° beam

   (3) 8"   lens   250- 750 watts 15-18° beam

   (4) 6"   lens   250- 750 watts 26-34° beam

   (5) 4½"   lens   250- 750 watts 40-45° beam

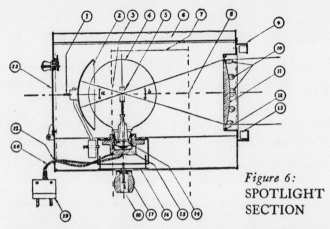

Figure 6:
SPOTLIGHT
SECTION

Section through a spotlight or lens hood, a typical construction diagram of an average spotlight. The solid lines with arrows indicate the typical direction of the rays of light. It will be noted that rays which emanate from the rear of the filament are reflected by a mirror so that they pass through the center of the filament toward the lens.

(1) *Reflector adjustment. Thumb screw.*

(2) *Spherical mirror.*

(3) *Sharp focus position for the lamp in relation to the lens.*

(4) *The globular (G-type) glass bulb of the lamp. This type is used exclusively in spotlights.*

(5) *Concentrated high-power filament burns base down to horizontal.*

(6) *Ventilating space.*

(7) *Focal range.*

(8) *Flood focus position for the filament.*

(9) *Horizontal color frame slides or grooves.*

(10) *Vent holes.*

(11) *Plano-convex lens.*

(12) *A spring ring used to hold the lens in position.*

(13) *Color frame clamp or spring.*

(14) *Base of the lamp.*

(15) *Socket, mounted in an adjustable lamp carriage which can be*

38

the spread is increased, so also the intensity decreases when the distance is increased and the spread is kept constant.

The figures here cited are based upon the assumption that the lamp is burning at full brightness, but for the sake of balancing the lighting or intensities on the various parts of the acting area, this is almost never the actual case. The number of dimmers on the control board should permit the dimming of each acting area spot individually to obtain this balance. When dimming an incandescent lamp, the intensity drops off quickly at the start of the traverse of the dimmer handle and slowly at the end. However, chiefly because the eye can notice differences of intensity at the low more readily than at the high end of the traverse of the dimmer, the effect to the eye is that of even dimming. Some people prefer to use one type of instrument with the same wattage lamp exclusively, instead of bothering to select precisely the wattage necessary. In this case, when high intensity is desired the number of units is increased, and where the opposite is desired the dimmer is used to

---

moved forward and backward to provide focal range.

(16) Focal slot.

(17) Focal handle, by which the position of the lamp in relation to the lens is regulated.

(18) Adjustment screw to raise or lower the socket.

(19) Male pin connector.

(20) Asbestos leads.

(21) Bushing.

(22) Access door, for removing and replacing the lamp and adjusting the reflector.

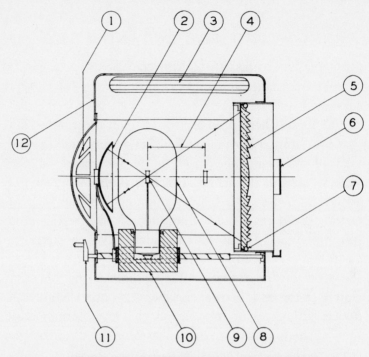

Figure 7: FRESNEL OR STEP-LENS SPOTLIGHT

Section through the spotlight showing structural features. The solid lines with arrows indicate the typical direction of rays.

    (1) Rear ventilator.
    (2) Spherical mirror.
    (3) Top vents.
    (4) Focal adjustment range.
    (5) Fresnel lens.
    (6) Color frame holder.
    (7) Spring ring to hold lens in position.
    (8) Bulb of T-type lamp to burn base down to horizontal.

    (9) Monoplane or biplane concentrated filament source.
    (10) Socket mounting on adjustable worm gear.
    (11) Focusing handle.
    (12) Access door—this lid raises to permit access to the lamp.

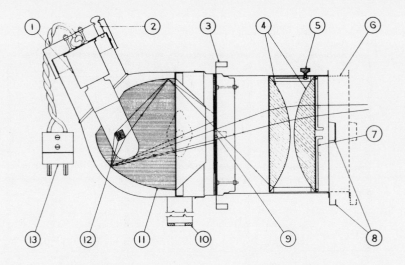

Figure 8: ELLIPSOIDAL REFLECTOR SPOTLIGHT
Section through spot showing the reflector and lens.

   (1) Medium Pre-focus Socket.
   (2) Socket Holder permitting removal of cap, socket, and lamp for re-lamping.
   (3) Push Shutter Handle.
   (4) Medium Focal Length Plano-Convex Lens.
   (5) Lens Adjustment Slide.
   (6) Lens Drum extended to front position.
   (7) Spring Ring Lens Holder.
   (8) Color Frame Holders.
   (9) Gate, generally about 3" in diameter.
  (10) Yoke.
  (11) Ellipsoidal reflector.
  (12) Concentrated filament.
  (13) Male Pin Connector.

41

Figure 9: SPOTLIGHT LENS CHARACTERISTICS

A diagrammatic indication of the manner in which lenses of different focal length (thickness) gather and converge the rays of light emanating from a concentrated source and the angle of the beam produced, due to the distance of the source from the lens. In the left-hand column the light source is at the front or "flood" focus, and in the right-hand column, the first two figures indicate the light at rear or "spot" focus. Note that a spherical reflector mounted at the rear of the source redirects the rays through the source when the centre of curvature of the reflector and the source coincide. In this way, the rays of light emanating from the back of the filament are redirected through the light source to the lens, and the amount of light in the beam is thereby increased from 25% to 50%.

A. Front position, no lens, direct emanation, 90 degree beam.

B. Rear position, no lens, 45 degree beam.

C. Front position, medium thick lens, 45 degree beam.

Note: The number of rays in the 90 degree angle emanating from the source are condensed into a 45 degree beam similar to a rear position source with no lens. (See "B".) The greater number of rays gathered by the lens gives correspondingly greater intensity of light in the beam.

D. Rear position, medium thick lens.

The source is now at the focal point of the lens. Therefore, the light rays in the 45 degree angle emanating from the source which is gathered by the lens emerge from the spotlight parallel to each other and give what is known as an intense "spot" of light.

E. Front position, thick lens.

Here the rays emanating from the source in a 90 degree angle are picked up by the lens and converged into a parallel beam, correspondingly brighter than "D". However, in practice the thick lens causes such irregularities in the beam and absorbs so much light, due to its thickness, that its advantage is almost completely offset.

F. Front position, Fresnel or step-lens.

This lens has the same gathering power as "E" because refraction is due primarily to the difference in angle between the two faces of the lens. Note that the curved segments of the step-lens follow precisely the curve of the thick lens indicated here by a dotted line. The disadvantage of thickness is hereby overcome so that the step-lens, when shaped to overcome irregularities in the beam, is the most efficient type made. Furthermore, the length of the spotlight hood can be reduced. T type lamp is necessary to obtain flood effect.

obtain the balance. Thus a 1000 watt spotlight can be used to obtain the range, not only normal to itself, but for any unit of lower wattage, or, two 1000 watt units partially down on dimmer can serve the same purpose as one 1500 watt spotlight. Nevertheless, the wisest course to follow lies in the selection of the instrument with the smallest wattage which will supply the range of intensity desired in view of all the variables, and whose maximum brightness when its dimmer is up full will give all the illumination that is needed in any scene.

The less regular variables that influence the intensity of light given by a spotlight are introduced by accessories that are applied to the instrument to make it more useful. A prefocus base lamp with a monoplane filament has been developed to guarantee the position of the filament in relation to the reflector and the lens by using a bayonet type of socket similar to that used in the automobile headlight lamp. In actual practice reflectors can increase the average intensity of the beam of light from 25 to 50 per cent, but this advantage is generally offset by the danger of double image due to the reflector's being off center (*Figure 10*). Reflectors can be recommended only for spotlights more or less permanently mounted or equipped with prefocus bases.

Spotlights are seldom used without some kind of color medium or diffuser. The total amount of intensity transmitted by diffusers is relatively high—between 85% and 95%—but as they spread the beam, in part, up to 180° the effective intensity in the useful direction may be less than 50%. Both glass and gelatin color mediums affect intensity enormously. The degree of this effect depends upon the purity of color from tints to hues and the opacity due to the graying effect of mixed pigments. The transmission of light is also dependent upon the color of the medium, since the incandescent filament is definitely richer in yellows and reds than it is in blue and it becomes distinctly redder as it is taken down on dimmer. The following is an approximate table of transmissions of a few of the various color mediums:

Pink	65%	Medium Green	18%
Magenta†	25%	Dark Green*	5%
Light Lavender	27%	Straw	85%
(Surprise Pink)		Light Amber	80%
Dark Lavender	15%	Medium Amber†	60%
Light Steel Blue	35%	Dark Amber	48%
Dark Steel Blue	20%	Light Scarlet	65%
Light Blue	20%	Light Red	30%
Medium Blue	10%	Medium Red	15%
Dark Blue*	3%	Dark Red*	10%
Blue-Green†	10%		

* Used as Primary Colors
† Used as Secondary Colors

These figures can only be taken very generally because no color mediums, even of the same lot, are exactly alike in color content, and the eye reacts very differently to different colors; it is more sensitive to the yellows and the greens which always appear brighter than the blues and reds.

The use of mats, flippers, funnels and cutoffs of all kinds (*Figure 11*), particularly when a diffusing medium is used, tends to cut down the effective intensity of

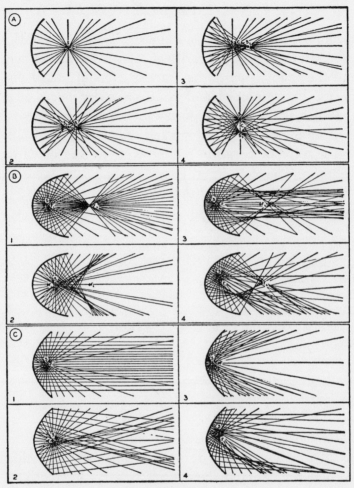

Figure 10

light from a spotlight. This is particularly marked when the beam is at wide spread with the intensity relatively low as a result, and an iris or a mat with a round hole is used to cut down the spread of the beam.

To sum up the variables involved in the selection of the wattage for an acting area spotlight, each may be considered in turn in respect to an illustrative problem.

1. The position of the instrument is determined, first, by the desired direction in which the beam of light is to fall on the acting area, in order to give the actor's

---

Figure 10: REFLECTOR SECTIONS

Three typical concave curved sections used in stage lighting instruments as a basis for controlling the rays of light. These are all symmetrical sections which, when developed into a three-dimensional form, have a circular face.

Number 1 in each case shows the position of the source at the optical centre and the direction of typical rays (at 10 degree intervals, representing all the rays that emanate from the source).

Number 2 indicates the effect when the source is outside or ahead of the optical centre.

Number 3 indicates the effect when it is behind or inside the optical centre.

Number 4 indicates the effect when the source is above the optical centre.

From these diagrams it is possible to trace the direction of reflected rays under all conditions and they are useful in analysing the direction of reflected rays from various portions of an enlarged light source—generally the case in practice.

A. Spherical reflectors used in lens hoods or spotlights.

B. Elliptical reflectors used in ellipsoidal reflector spotlights and floodlights.

C. Parabolic reflectors used in projectors and border lights.

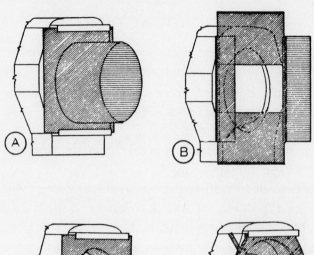

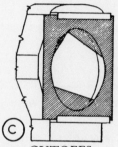

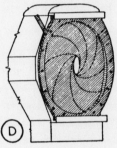

Figure 11: CUTOFFS

Accessories used on the front of instruments to control the spread of light. Usually they are painted a dull black so that they reflect as little light as possible and confine the rays to the proper area, thus cutting off some of the normal spread of light.

A. The typical funnel. Generally used in connection with a diffusing screen to prevent the diffuse light from spilling.

B. A flipper shutter. An adjustable cutoff used to give the beam a rectangular form. Most often used on instruments lighting the acting area from the front of the balcony.

C. Mat. Black cardboard or metal mat generally mounted in a color frame with the color medium, to shape the beam.

D. Iris. A means of varying the size of the beam spread.

48

face the best visibility and plastic quality, and second, by the available structural arrangements which will permit mounting the instrument to give as nearly as possible this direction to the rays of light.

2. The position establishes the distance and to some extent the spread of light. It may be assumed that a 20′ throw and a 20° beam has been determined by the ground plan of the setting and the size of the area to be lighted. At this distance, with this spread, a 1000 watt spotlight will give about 25 foot-candles of illumination.

3. The color medium with its diffuser transmits 50% of the light rays so that the intensity of illumination is cut down to 12½ f.c. If the background is dark this will give adequate visibility illumination; in fact, it may produce a glare due to too much contrast.

Experience will soon indicate the wattage necessary for acting area spotlights, and the variables will be considered unconsciously in view of the numerous other problems that are presented.

COLOR

The color of the acting area lights must give the actor's face a slightly exaggerated effect which is consistent with his character and the motivation of the lighting. It is no longer necessary to use make-up to offset the unnatural direction, color and distribution of strong footlights and borders. Make-up assists in defining the character that the actor portrays, and lighting should not destroy this effect, but since the color of the light affects the appearance of pigment considerably it is necessary to have the color of the make-up and the light supplement each other. It is possible to select color mediums that give the made-up face a very complimentary appearance; it is also possible to achieve the reverse.

The color of the light is further determined by the attempt to be consistent with the motivating light, such as sunlight, moonlight, gaslight, etc. Motivating light should more or less substantiate the amount of illumination necessary for the acting areas, and in turn, it is wise to let the acting area illumination be of the color and amount that would be given by natural sources. Thus the color of the make-up may have to be adjusted to the light used to co-ordinate with the motivating source. This will be understood best by experimenting with make-ups used under moonlight.

The color of the acting area light also affects the appearance of costumes, but by balancing the acting area lights, or using the toning lights, costumes can be made to appear as they were designed. A blue costume seen in the yellow rays of the setting sun and the amber of the acting area lights that go with it, will probably appear as a lifeless gray unless acting area light from another direction, or the general toning light, has some blue in it to pick up the color of the costume.

When cross lighting is used on each acting area, to provide plasticity and proper visibility to the actor's face, those instruments focused in a direction which is consistent with the motivating light will normally be of the same color as the motivating light. This naturally suggests the use of the complementary color from the opposite direction. If warm color is used from one side, cool color can be used from the other, just as the cool blue of daylight appears in the shadows caused by the warm rays from the sun.

The effect of using a warm and cool color from opposite sides on each acting area strikes at the root of another make-up practice; that of using purple or blue lines or shading to give the effect of wrinkles or hollows on the face. The real problem of make-up is to provide certain lines and shadows that make parts of the face reflect less light than other parts, so that the reflecting character of the make-up is important, and not its actual color. Since purple and blue lines have the same reflecting value in a cool-colored light as the ordinary flesh tints, black or gray make-up should be used for wrinkles and hollows and should be used with lighter base color for high lighting.

Ordinarily the face of the actor should appear normal. It is obvious that except for spectacular effects the color used in the acting area light should be just off white—a warm or cool *tint*, rather than a pure color. In general, greens, blues and reds should be avoided and ambers, pinks, and lavenders or steel blues used. These colors will give the face tone and will not distort it. They will also tend to promote visibility because objects can be seen more clearly under tints than under pure colors.

The most practical advantage in their use lies in the fact that tinted color mediums transmit more light than the deep colors and thus make the acting area spotlights more efficient. Deep colors, unless carefully selected, are as apt to distort the appearance of a costume as to enhance it, and in the same sense the tints tend to dilute the color effect of a costume. When great richness of color is desired in the acting area, obviously, some means of lighting the face of the actor separately must be provided.

DISTRIBUTION

The distribution of light over the acting area should give what might be called dramatic visibility. Some areas are obviously more important than others and sometimes the best visibility from a dramatic point of view is that which does not allow too clear a delineation of form. The balance of intensity on the various areas depends primarily upon the working out of the business of the actor. The purpose of dividing the acting area into small sections is to permit flexibility of visibility and emphasis over the various parts of the stage. Occasionally directors wish to suppress the arbitrary nature of acting area spotlighting and are willing to confine the action to areas lighted by only a few of the acting area lights, or even to depend upon the motivating light (provided it is adequate to give good visibility) during the important scenes. This method requires the minimum layout of equipment and it may be the goal toward which the director and technician should strive, but until directors are able to visualize the effect of lighting while they are working out the business of a scene, it is wiser to provide adequate visibility over the entire acting area by the illumination from units that perform this function alone. Spotlighting only certain pieces of furniture and entrances and then relying upon the brightness of the border lights to fill in the gaps, does not provide enough flexibility, nor does it ordinarily simplify the amount of equipment necessary.

Visibility lighting is, at best, arbitrary and at odds with a naturalistic effect so that every effort should be made to make it as natural as possible. Light, directed from the footlights, or even from the first border, is apt to be bad. Beams of light from directly overhead cause deep shadows on the face, and from the center front of the balcony they tend to eliminate all form by allowing no highlights and shadows, which are valuable contributions to our conception of the solidity of objects in space (*Figure 12*).

As long ago as the Renaissance it was discovered that the best balance of light and shade to promote the effect of plasticity could be obtained by considering sunlight falling diagonally, from over one shoulder. Such diagonal lighting has been taken as a convention by architects in making renderings of their projects to show the best indication of solid forms.

Next to the delineation given by differences in brightness, outline and color, the light and shade on an object

Figure 12: A CUBE UNDER DIFFERENT DIRECTIONS
AND DISTRIBUTIONS OF LIGHT

(1) General distribution, light coming from all directions, thus practically eliminating the form of the cube.

(2) Direct down light such as might be given by a lens hood mounted directly above the acting area. Very little illumination on the vertical faces.

(3) Centre frontal lighting, as from the front of the balcony, showing the position in which a shadow falls on the back wall, directly behind the cube.

give the clearest sense of plasticity; that is, the position of objects in relation to each other and their solidity of form. The sense of plasticity beyond the limits of stereoscopic vision (about fifty feet) is due primarily to the direction and distribution of light. Plasticity is best achieved when the direction of the light is at 45° in plan and elevation along a diagonal drawn between the extreme corners of a cube (*Figures 1, 2 and 3*).

Thus, if light is directed to the acting area as nearly as possible along the diagonal of a cube the actor will be

---

(4) Side lighting, as from the tormentor, showing the long shadow, only fair top lighting, and giving sharp contrast between the two vertical faces of the cube.

(5) Centre front at a 45 degree angle, showing equal illumination to the two faces of the cube and a less distracting shadow than in diagram 3.

(6) Side lighting at 45 degrees, showing good top lighting and illumination to one of the vertical faces, and a reasonable position for the shadow.

(7) Back lighting. Showing good top lighting and separation from the background by reason of contrast and therefore used considerably in motion picture work, but giving poor illumination to the two vertical faces.

(8) Front lighting from below as from a footlight spot, showing the exaggerated effect of the shadow, no light on top, and equal illumination of the two vertical faces.

(9) Diagonal lighting, giving a desirable balance of highlight and shadow. This is the convention used by architects in rendering their drawings.

made more visible and sculpturesque than if he is lighted from any other direction. But, unless specially planned, the business and positions of the actor make it as necessary for him to face away from this direction as into it. As a result it has been found wise to light each area from the two diagonals with respect to the direction in which the audience is facing (*Figure 4*). It may be pointed out that the use of two directions tends to limit the plastic quality that would be given by one. This is true. It is chiefly for the sake of giving adequate visibility to the actor when he faces away from the direction of the dominant lighting that this extra source is used. By using warm and cool colors on opposite sides and varying the intensity between the two, it is possible to retain a considerable amount of the plastic quality. Moreover, this arrangement guarantees the visibility of the actor's face no matter in which direction he turns. Under any condition the shadow side of an object should be illuminated to some extent by the complementary of the predominating color, just as daylight gives a cool light in the shadows caused by the sun.

Those instruments which direct their rays on the acting area at approximately the same direction as the motivating light, can be of high intensity and of the same color as the motivating source. The direction of the sunlight into a room from the left would indicate that all the left hand acting area lights should be bright and equipped with white or amber color mediums. The right hand side would be lower in intensity and white or cool in color. White is considered in both cases here because it tends to give the opposite effect to that produced by either a warm or a cool color. If the motivating light comes from a fixture in the center of the room, all those spotlights which direct their rays to the acting area from that direction should be warm, and the others cool. Where there are no special instruments used as motivating sources, the acting area lights from one or both sides can serve as such.

It has been pointed out that the direction of light rays establishes a certain position for the instrument. The conventional methods of building theatres and scenery limit this position considerably; in fact, in most theatres and with most scenery, it is impossible even to approach the ideal of directing light to the acting area along the diagonal of a cube. And even when the stage and auditorium are planned to allow for the intelligent placing of instruments, scenery is seldom designed to allow for mounting them in any but the conventional positions. Flexibility of position is necessary because no two settings for the same stage are apt to be alike in form. The diagrams given here may seem to indicate a standard position for each acting area spotlight, but this is not intended. For most interior sets the positions are, however, more or less the same, particularly for those instruments used to light the front of the stage.

Except for unusual productions the instruments should be concealed from the audience. This further limits their possible positions. The diagonal of a cube

projected from the center of each of the suggested acting areas on the stage toward the auditorium will strike
the walls and ceiling of the auditorium at the ideal
positions for mounting each of the acting area spotlights
(*Figure 2*). It will be found that the front areas of the
stage should be lighted from the ceiling, high up on the
side walls, or the face of the second balcony in the auditorium. Under some conditions the left hand spot on
the down-stage left area may be mounted close at hand
behind the left tormentor (*Figure 1*). The same is true
on stage right, but proximity to the area lighted tends
to give an artificial effect. The face of the ordinary balcony, even from the sides, generally provides too low
an angle. The up-stage, or three rear areas, can usually
be lighted from the stage side of the proscenium. The
general mounting locations· should be numerous and
large enough to allow considerable latitude in the actual
placing of the instruments for the different scenes; they
should be accessible for changing color mediums and
focusing.

Having determined the position for the instruments,
the distance to the area lighted is correspondingly fixed.
By referring to the tables of intensities (page 35) for
the wattage necessary within the range of throw, the
size of lamp and the instrument itself can be selected.
The six areas in the general acting space are determined
as much to meet the characteristic spread and intensity
of the spotlight as they are to promote flexibility. The
spread over one area is the widest angle that the ordinary

spotlight can give effectively. Thus, for small stages, fewer areas can be used and for larger stages several more, but as the number of units is increased the complication of control is also increased, so that the six divisions may be considered a happy medium.

In this method of lighting, the illumination of the areas should overlap sufficiently so that there are no "dead pockets" through which the actor must walk. If the business does not take the actor too close to the setting, it is usually (but not always) possible to keep the acting area lights from falling on the scenery. The shadow of the actor moving against the scenery is bound to be distracting. If, on the other hand, the beam of a spotlight is allowed to fall on the scenery or even on the floor of the stage, it gives a sharp oval pool of light unless the edge is softened by the use of a diffusing medium.

By the use of either diffusers or step lenses the pools of light are blended into the rest of the lighting and the acting areas are pulled together. This practice, however, dissipates somewhat the control of the direction of light so that it may fall on parts of the scenery and auditorium which should not be lighted. The spill, or stray light, caused by the diffusing medium can be eliminated by the use of a funnel on the spotlight, but the funnel must be unduly long if the spill is to be entirely cut off.

A practical method of soft edging a beam of a plano convex spotlight is to scratch the edge of the color medium, or to oil the center of a frost gelatin, so that the normal transmission in the center of the beam is maintained.

Great care must be taken to keep the light rays where they are wanted. Since the acting areas are actually neither round nor elliptical, nor is the scenery constructed on curved lines so that it will fit the normal shape of the beam from a spotlight, the form of the light beam (the normal cone of light created by the lens) must often be shaped by cutoffs, i.e., funnels, mats, flippers, shutters, etc. (*Figure 11*). On a brightly lighted set this problem is not important, but cutoffs of some kind to shape the beam of light are often necessary accessories to the acting area spotlights.

It is possible to obtain a sharp control over the form of light given by a spotlight only with the ellipsoidal type (*Figure 8*). This unit provides maximum flexibility, and more control than any other type of instrument except the "effect machine" (stereopticon), or the Linnebach lantern (shadow projector), which produces precise patterns.

In practice ellipsoidal spots are invariably used as "front" lights (in front of the proscenium) and generally fresnels behind because of their natural soft edge.

It is obvious that unless a great many instruments are used the direction of each one is important. Some spotlights are equipped with sticky universal joints that permit turning the instrument through a wide angle, and holding it in whatever position it is set (*Figure 13*).

CONTROL

Control of the light illuminating the acting area, as for all other lighting, involves the control of intensity, color, distribution, and changes. After each acting area spotlight has been focused and its beam directed to cover the required area, it is possible to compose the stage picture from the switchboard by varying the intensity of each unit separately. This assumes that there is a separate dimmer for each unit. If cool light comes from one direction and warm from another, emphasis can be given to either by the simple process of dimming from the switchboard. When the proper balance of intensities has been determined each dimmer will probably have a different reading because of the unequal distances of throw and the differences of emphasis and color desired for each area. Occasionally the acting area lights can be grouped so that two or more are controlled by the same dimmer, which should be of proper size or capacity to handle the load. In this way the number of controls is reduced, but flexibility of control is also limited.

The building up of a definite lighting distribution, or the balancing of intensities, is a little like modelling in clay. Giving form to all the visual elements on the stage is part of the procedure for a lighting rehearsal (arranged before the dress rehearsal), where everything except the actor should be present.

For most scenes, the acting area lights do not change during the scene. The intensities at which the acting

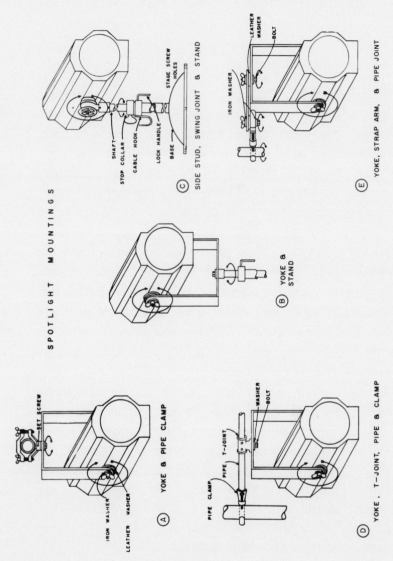

SPOTLIGHT MOUNTINGS

Ⓐ YOKE & PIPE CLAMP

IRON WASHER
LEATHER WASHER
SET SCREW

Ⓑ YOKE & STAND

Ⓒ SIDE STUD, SWING JOINT & STAND

SHAFT
STOP COLLAR
CABLE HOOK
LOCK HANDLE
BASE
STAGE SCREW HOLES

Ⓓ YOKE, T-JOINT, PIPE & CLAMP

PIPE CLAMP
PIPE
T-JOINT
WASHER
BOLT

Ⓔ YOKE, STRAP ARM, & PIPE JOINT

LEATHER WASHER
BOLT
IRON WASHER

Figure 13

area lights are set are recorded on a set-up sheet which is a record of the position of each switch and a reading for each dimmer used in the scene. The set-up sheet is not to be confused with the cue sheet which records lighting changes (usually confined to motivating and background lights) which occur during the scene.

Movement is possible with lighting to a limited degree. Abstractly, changes of light can be perceived more readily than changes in sound, but our knowledge of instruments and light, and our light sense, are not yet developed to the point of establishing lighting as an art form in the same terms as music.

Figure 13: TYPES OF MOUNTINGS
Planes of rotation indicated by arrows. Lens instruments illustrated in A to E are generally mounted with a universal joint—two planes of rotation perpendicular to each other—so that they can be focused in a variety of directions.

Generally the joints should be tight and sticky, so that the instrument can be redirected and will retain its new position. Joints are made tight by the use of leather or spring washers. Generally the joint should be tightened by a wing nut or thumb bolt, although in a number of cases a set screw or a nut is provided to insure a permanent mounting.

A. Horizontal pipe mountings.

B and C are stand and base mountings, generally used on the floor. In this respect they are portable unless, for the sake of security, they are screwed to the floor or the surface on which they are mounted.

D and E. Vertical pipe batten mountings, such as might be found at the tormentor.

Eventually each change in situation during a scene may be enhanced by changes in lighting. Most attempts to do this now with the average type of switchboard require endless rehearsal and in the end are apt to be distracting. But slow, subtle changes as in a sunset and sunrise can be simulated on the stage if great care is taken. The distribution of light at any moment in a change should be considered in terms of a static effect, recordable as a definite group of dimmer readings. This is all the more important in view of the fact that the switchboard operator is not always able to see the effects which he is creating for an audience. Most switchboards with a sufficient number of dimmers are adequate pieces of apparatus to provide a static set-up, but the problem of making proportional time changes on them implies presetting dimmer readings and fading from one set-up to another.

With a striplight having two or more color circuits it is possible to create a change of color by dimming the intensity of one or all of the circuits up or down, but with a spotlight (a single source unit) the range of color control is definitely limited. Of course, it is possible to change color mediums between scenes, if the instrument is accessible. The Europeans employ a method of changing color mediums mechanically by pulling the color medium across the face of the instrument with a wire cable operated over a series of pulleys from the switchboard. Our own manufacturers have developed an electro-magnetic color control for pulling the color medium over the face of the instrument or allowing it to drop clear of the beam. With neither of these methods is the change subtle. The spotlight has not yet been developed which will give as good a range of color control as can now be had with a striplight. Double or triple sets of instruments are sometimes installed to give a color range desired.

As a rule, only floor units are changed in position from scene to scene. Hanging units can be taken up or down. If accessible, the direction and even the shape of the beam of the spotlight can be changed by hand for each new scene. The best example of control over the distribution of light is the hand-operated, high-powered arc follow spotlight often found in the projection booth. But these instruments are not particularly useful in legitimate plays because they are not under control from the switchboard operator. Some attempts have been made to control the direction and spread of spotlights by means of remotely controlled motors, but the apparatus is too expensive for ordinary use. For the present, changes of distribution from the acting area spotlights during a scene are limited to a variation of the intensity or to hand operation at the instrument.

BLENDING AND TONING

ACTING area lights are used primarily to illuminate the acting area and insure visibility there. They are adjusted to give the proper dramatic composition to the actor's positions on the stage. In addition, the stage space and the background immediately surrounding the acting area must be illuminated somewhat in the manner in which daylight accompanies the direct rays of the sun. The lighting is soft and general in distribution, blending the whole visual aspect and toning in atmospheric quality the surroundings against which the important character or object is seen.

Theoretically the blending and tonal lighting of the stage is general and shadowless in distribution and variable only in intensity and color. Practically it is impossible to obtain such distribution under any conditions. The best instruments to use for blending and toning are three (or four) color striplights (*Figure 14*). A large bank of lights with a large diffusing screen covering them would give a better distribution than striplights do, because striplights give general distribution only along one axis. However, since mounting space and openings in the set are limited, striplights seem to be the best instruments to use. Obviously the most important position from which to direct general light into the

Figure 14: BORDERLIGHTS
Borderlight strips, hung over the stage parallel to the proscenium.

A. *Compartment type, using specially shaped chromium or etched aluminum reflectors of a compact type. Generally built to use colored glass roundels, but often furnished with color frame slides for the use of gelatin. Built specially for each wattage lamp from 50 to 1000 watts, more generally furnished in the 200 watt size.*

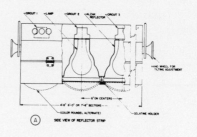

(A)   SIDE VIEW OF REFLECTOR STRIP

B. *Reflector lamp strip, consisting of a row of sockets in a partially compartmentalized metal hood using reflector floods or spots in the PAR or R-40 type, generally 150 watts although 75 watt and 300 watt lamps are available. Glass color filters are most practical to resist heat and fading.*

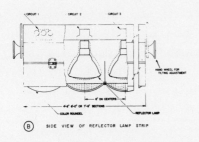

(B)   SIDE VIEW OF REFLECTOR LAMP STRIP

---

stage space is behind the frame of the proscenium. Thus border lights and footlights (occasionally proscenium strips) best serve the purpose. The former, when employed with a box set, are generally used to blend the acting areas together. In an exterior scene which uses cloth borders, strips are used both as blending and toning instruments and in this case several rows of such lights may be useful. The instruments used to light the backdrop or cyclorama and all those parts not immediately surrounding the acting area are considered separately in the next chapter. Footlights should serve primarily as tonal units which project a low general illumination on the set and illuminate the shadows caused by the directional effect of motivating, border, or acting area lighting.

BORDERLIGHTS

The rows of lamps mounted in long metal hoods and hung in the fly space over the stage floor are remnants of the days when numerous small sources, similarly mounted, were required to give intensity of illumination. A great number of sources lighted the scenery and the actor equally from all directions so that there always seemed to be a need for more light. The invention of the incandescent lamp seemed to supply this need but it was soon discovered that the amount of illumination did not make visibility proportionally greater. The value of contrast in the illumination of the various parts of the stage has made great intensities from the borderlights unnecessary. The use of individual, shaped reflectors, shadow boxes, and dense color mediums which permit greater control over the distribution of light from border strips, tends to demand equal or greater initial power in the source than was necessary with the old open type strips.

The intensity of light given by borderlights can in all cases be less than that of the acting area lights, because contrast is a necessary contribution to visibility. In the same sense the amount of light needed to blend the various acting areas is apt to be more than that required to light the setting. The days when footlights and borderlights were the chief sources of illumination are fortunately past, but the tradition seems to hold over, since most equipment manufacturers insist on installing a complete complement of several rows of high-powered borderlights and often a double row of footlights. In fact many producers, particularly those who stage musical and presentation shows, think high-powered footlights and borderlights are necessary means of giving glamour to the stage picture.

Borderlights are space-filling lighting instruments. The more space the greater is the intensity required. Their effect is noticed chiefly by the amount of illumination they give to the acting area, so that the wattage required depends on the area and length of the throw. Each circuit of lamps in the strip should be able to deliver up to ten foot-candles of illumination on the acting area after the absorption of color mediums has been discounted. From one to five foot-candles is usually adequate if the acting area is lighted by several border strips and acting area lights, but where a single border strip, insufficient acting area lights and dense color mediums are used, the higher figure is more usually correct. The figures in the appended table are more or less hypothetical and should be applied with a great deal of flexibility in view of the variables involved. They are based primarily upon experience in the use of different sized proscenium openings. If the figure for each height is multiplied by the proscenium width, the total wattage normally necessary for each color circuit in the first border can be computed.

Teaser Height	10′	15′	20′	25′
Total Watts per Foot of Proscenium Width	20	40	60	80

It is seldom necessary or advisable to use a border strip the full width of the proscenium, but the total wattage should be the same irrespective of the length of the strip. The first border hung just behind the teaser is more important and requires more wattage than those used farther upstage because it is the only one which can be used when there is a ceiling on the setting. The rear border, when there are several, is generally used for lighting the backdrop or cyclorama and is considered with background lights in another chapter.

One of the chief characteristics of a borderlight is its ability to give a variety of color tone over the acting area. The borderlight is a more or less standard piece of equipment. It is used to light almost every type of scene, and is generally wired in three color circuits so that a variety of colors can be obtained by varying the

intensity of light from the different color circuits. Theoretically the primary colors of light—red, green, and
blue—when used simultaneously or individually at various intensities, will give almost the complete range of
color tones distinguishable by the eye; but these color
mediums cut off so much light that they are relatively
inefficient for blending purposes. It is wise to select
either the lighter tints of these same shades or to determine just what three tints of color are going to be
necessary, individually or in combination in all the scenes
for the particular production, or to add a fourth circuit
of white to the primaries.

Glass roundels are now made commercially in shades
of amber, surprise pink, green-blue, and the primaries,
red, green and blue. Gelatin, although it tends to fade
under the heat of the lamp (glass does not) is made in a
sufficient variety of colors to warrant its use when special
tints are desired. For this reason the borderlight strip
should be made to take gelatins as well as glass. Also,
since most strips are made with individual reflectors,
closely spaced, to accommodate from 100 to 500 watt
lamps, dipped or coated lamps are out of the question.
Even for the strips built to use lamps below 40 watts
(the largest that can be dipped), roundels and color
mediums, or natural color lamps which have the color
blown in the glass bulb are more satisfactory than dipped
bulbs.

Great improvements have been made recently in the

construction and form of the borderlight strip. The old open metal troughs with closely spaced, low wattage lamps have been replaced by higher powered lamps in individual, etched aluminum or shiny Alzak specially shaped reflectors for narrow beam distribution.

One disadvantage of the newer borderlight is that, when it is wired for four colors, it requires large lamps and correspondingly large reflectors. Similar colors are apt to be spaced so far apart that the effect of general distribution is given only when the distance to the area lighted is great and the number of units is sufficient to prevent a spotty distribution. This is not serious except when a cloth border hangs close to the strip and the total wattage has been divided between too few units; then poor distribution of color from the borderlights is particularly apparent.

Usual commercial practice is to standardize on 200 watt reflector units up to a 20′ teaser height, with 300 and 500 watt sizes for the very large stages. Only in musical comedy, opera, and presentation productions where cloth borders and wings are usually used, are several rows of border strips extending the full width of the proscenium needed. In the majority of legitimate staging, the first borderlight and perhaps another for lighting the backdrop are the only strips required above the stage and the former need not be longer than half the width of the proscenium (*Figure 2, XR*).

Figure 14B. Reflector lamp strips are compact and

highly efficient compartment units built on 6" centers for up to 300 W R-40 lamps—flood or spot types and on 8" or 9" centers for 300 W PAR or 500 W R-40 types also in spot or flood form. 3 or 4 color circuits are customary and thus portable units are 6 to 8 feet long. Glass color filters in plain, stripped or spread roundel form are required. This limits the color choice considerably and is chiefly responsible for the slow acceptance of this type of strip.

When the theatre is equipped with curtains made up of borders and wings, the practice of installing a border strip back of each cloth border in addition to the first border in the initial layout is required; but this practice is too often overdone and more useful equipment has to be omitted on account of budget limitations. If the theatre is to be used for musical shows and operas occasionally, extra border strips in portable form (sections 4' to 8' long) can always be hung in their proper place and removed when they are not needed.

The use of outlets on wire ways or pipes hung above the stage in the place of borders allows for the use of spotlights and floodlights from traditional borderlight positions. In fact even the first border strip can be made in portable sections because there are times when it is not needed. If the border strips are made portable, the "worklight" circuit which is generally incorporated in each borderlight should be retained to feed separate units either mounted permanently on the border strip battens or wherever they will be effective in lighting the stage for scene shifts. On large stages the practice of breaking long borderlights into sections for the sake of control of distribution may offer certain advantages, but it also complicates the control at the switchboard. As long as borderlights are used primarily to tone and blend the lighting on the acting area this refinement is not often practical.

One or two large floods in each of the chosen colors can often take the place of borderlights for toning purposes. The shadows of the actors will fall on the floor and with a box set great care should be taken to keep the direct rays from the borderlights off the scenery. Only where border and wing sets are used should borderlights serve to light the setting. For this reason long borderlight strips are useless and those who have them should unscrew the end lamps so that only the center portion remains lighted. A set of lightspill shields, called a shadow box, hung from the first border is sometimes used to keep the light from spilling on the side and rear walls of the setting.

The position of the first borderlight, or concert border, often called the "X-rays" (the trade name of a glass store-window reflector that was used formerly in stage borderlights), should be as close to the bottom edge of the teaser as possible without being visible. A box teaser or thickness piece (*Figures 15, 16 and 17*) masks the teaser lights, allows a lower trim for the borderlights or a higher trim for the teaser and thus permits the

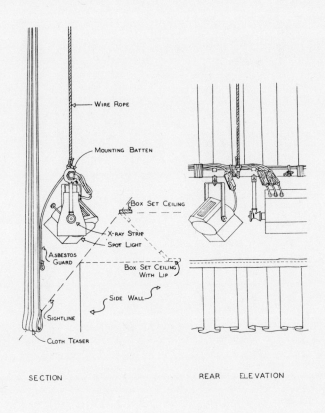

WIRE ROPE

MOUNTING BATTEN

BOX SET CEILING

X-RAY STRIP
SPOT LIGHT

ASBESTOS
GUARD

BOX SET CEILING
WITH LIP

SIDE WALL

SIGHTLINE

CLOTH TEASER

SECTION

REAR   ELEVATION

Figure 15: TEASER MOUNTINGS: A.

Simple Cloth Teaser with Asbestos Guard.

This is the typical professional method of mounting the border lights and border spotlights. A box set must be from 3' to 4' higher than the teaser in order to give proper masking. A ceiling with a front lip allows for reducing this height considerably.

75

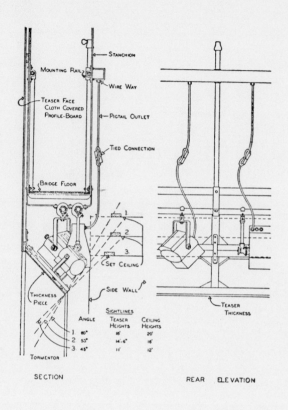

Figure 16: TEASER MOUNTINGS: B.
Thickness Piece or Portal Method.
The table of sight lines indicates the relation between teaser heights and ceiling heights. The setting with this method needs to be less than two feet higher than the teaser.

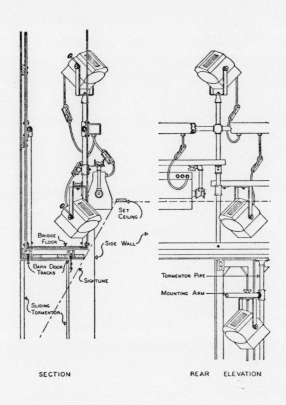

SET
CEILING

BRIDGE
FLOOR

SIDE WALL

BARN DOOR
TRACKS

SIGHTLINE

SLIDING
TORMENTOR

TORMENTOR PIPE

MOUNTING ARM

SECTION   REAR   ELEVATION

Figure 17: TEASER MOUNTINGS: C.
Bridge Thickness Piece with Adjustable Tormentor Tower.
The advantage of mounting instruments above the bridge floor
lies in the accessability of instruments for focusing and changing
color mediums.

77

audience to see more of the ceiling of the setting. Additional borderlights are generally spaced on seven foot centers and hung parallel to the proscenium because this arrangement conforms to the traditional spacing for wings and scenery borders.

The range of intensity of illumination that should be provided by borderlights is debatable. It is certain, however, that where directed, controlled illumination is given by other instruments, the use of border strips is correspondingly less important and relegated to giving a low general illumination that can blend the spotlighted areas together in a range of color tones. With all the color circuits burning at the greatest intensity or "full up", it is possible to "cut" one or more circuits by switch or to dim any or all of them to any degree on the dimmers. Changes in color are accomplished by this method. Inefficient as the primary colors are, they will give the greatest range of tonality by the addition of one to the other at varying intensities. Without a thorough knowledge of the principles of color mixing the trial and error method will have to be used and this is even more true when four colors or colors that are not primaries are employed. Some technicians advocate the use of focusing borderlights that can be directed to cover areas where the light is needed. Ideally a focusing borderlight is a desirable unit, but it increases the cost and control of what is normally only supposed to be a blending and toning instrument. Borderlights can be tipped up or

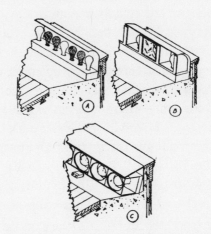

Figure 18:
FOOTLIGHTS

A. Old type open trough, using closely spaced, low wattage, dipped or natural color lamps.
B. Compartment type footlight using high-wattage lamps with color frames and equipped with color frame slides.
C. The compact, specially shaped reflector strip, using glass roundels and 50, 100 or 150 watt lamps, generally 100. The pin connector pigtail is used to feed footlight spots.

down to extend their illumination over various depths of the stage space and can be raised or lowered to correspond with the height of the setting.

FOOTLIGHTS

Footlights (*Figure 18*), like borderlights, have come down from the time when the theatre was first taken indoors and every available position was used to project light into the stage space. They are so essentially artificial in their effect that they have become almost symbolic of all that is meant by "Theatre". They are still very useful, though modern practice has somewhat altered their function and limited their duties. The great cry against them raised by some critics is valid only in cases in which footlights are used as blatantly as they were when there was no other means of lighting the actor at the front of the stage. Musical comedy methods often call for the greatest amount of light possible from the footlights, but in legitimate production footlights should be used to illuminate the shadows on the actors' faces and to tone the setting at low intensity. In this respect footlights are very useful and the practice of omitting them from a layout only limits the flexibility of stage lighting.

Another very practical use of footlights is to illuminate the act curtain as the house lights are taken down in order to draw the attention of the audience to the stage. This can also be done with the front acting area lights or by means of special instruments mounted on the face of the balcony, and to some extent the setting can be toned by the direct rays from the blending and acting area lights and the reflected rays from the floor of the stage. But in spite of the more limited function of footlights, their installation and restricted use is recommended.

The possible intensity of light that can be obtained from footlights is limited by the space allowed for them. Footlights should not rise above the level of the stage floor more than three inches because they tend to cut off the view of the stage floor for those sitting in the front rows of the auditorium. High wattage footlights are required only by the musical show. The range of intensity for each footlight color circuit may vary from a fraction of a foot-candle of illumination to something less than ten, discounting the absorption of the color mediums used. Broadly speaking, from 25 to 50 watts per color per foot of proscenium width ought to give an adequate range of intensity. This wattage may be in the form of natural colored lamps (25 and 40 watts standard), or the regular white lamp from 25 to 200 watts (100 watt size generally) in individual reflectors which use roundels or gelatin.

Footlights should give a lower general blend of color tone than the borderlights because the effect of light from the footlights is seen very readily on the setting. This is particularly true if footlights are the only light source for illuminating the setting. There must be at least ten lamps or sources of the same color burning simultaneously in order to eliminate shadows. The colors to be used in the three color circuits are somewhat similar to those used in the borderlights except that red, green, and blue, in spite of their low transmission, will give the deep colors and, when used in combinations, even the tints desired.

Footlights should give general shadowless illumination in any tone. As far as possible within their confined space they should approach the effect of a line of light for each of the colors. To accomplish this the lamps should be as close together as possible. In some respects the neon tube gives the closest approximation to the line source. Where two small lamps can give the same wattage as a larger lamp in about the same space it is wiser to use the small lamps. Some footlight strips are constructed with two rows of lamps but this type of installation is generally unnecessary for legitimate theatres. The individual reflector type, although it requires larger spacing than the continuous trough, is more efficient in projecting the light back into the stage space.

One instrument for obtaining good mixing and an apparent continuous line source is an indirect footlight strip. The intensity with this unit is cut down to about 50% of that available from the direct type of footlight but it gives good results where the intensity can be low.

The footlight strip should be so hooded that its rays are all directed into the setting and none are allowed to fall outside the proscenium opening. This seems to be an obvious suggestion but it is astonishing how few footlight strips are properly shielded. The strip should include all the wattage necessary according to the estimates cited, in a hood about 75% of the width of the proscenium opening. It is always distracting to see the setting lighted brightly where is meets the proscenium. In order to prevent a shadow of the edge of the foot-

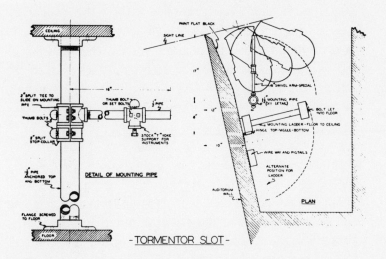

Figure 19:
TORMENTOR SLOT

Method of mounting side spotlights at the proscenium in a slot or behind a moving tower. The yoke of the spotlight is suspended from the slider on the pipe arm. Thumb bolts on the slider, swivel arm, pipe and stop collar permit fixing the position of the spotlight manually.

---

light pit, the construction of the strip should be compact enough to allow the filament of the lamps to be on line with the floor and yet not have its protecting hood more than three inches above the level of the stage.

The practice of dividing and controlling the footlights in sections, particularly for the purpose of making them fold into the floor easily, carries with it the danger of interrupting the line of light and leaving too few units to give shadowless illumination. When the shadows of the actors can be seen moving across the back wall of the setting there are too few sources in the footlights as well as too much intensity. A simple method of dividing the footlight strip is to provide three sections, the center as long as the two ends together, and controlling each one separately or the two ends as one (*Figure 2, FL*). The centre section is decidedly the most useful and by an arrangement of switches it is possible to cut off the end sections and still use only one dimmer for each color circuit for the whole strip. If each section is to be controlled separately there must be three times the number of dimmers available. In most musical show houses four or five current outlets are installed in the strip to feed footlight spotlights when they are wanted.

All of the types of footlights so far discussed are sunk in a fireproofed pit at the front edge of the stage (the "apron"). While it is advisable to build the fixed or disappearing type in permanently, the footlight pit is occasionally useful for instruments that give a special distribution of light. If the strip is made in portable sections it can be removed to make place for special instruments and it can be used elsewhere if the supply of strips is limited.

The control of light from the footlight position is

somewhat similar to that provided for the borderlights. Where there is adequate front lighting at a good angle the light from footlights is needed only to illuminate the setting or can even be dispensed with entirely if there is sufficient spill from the borders and reflected light from the floor to perform this function. If there are no front lights the footlight intensity must be correspondingly greater to help illuminate the actor's face. In this case the setting must be lighted somewhat by the overhead borders to help balance the shadows that may fall on the back wall. The balance of illumination from footlights and borders must also eliminate the apparent artificiality of the directional light from the footlights. The most noticeable effect of the illumination from the footlight position occurs on the large expanse of the background or setting. Footlights can provide an amazing range of color tonality of the proper dramatic character, but, when used carelessly, they may ruin a night sky or even the painting of the setting. When the footlights are divided into separately controlled sections it is possible to tone the different parts of the setting and to get some variety of tonality over the acting area. The wide spread of light from each section, however, limits this practice.

LIGHTING BACKGROUND SURFACES

UP TO this point the acting area and the parts of the setting immediately surrounding it have been considered. That part of the stage seen beyond is called "background" for the sake of convenience. Backgrounds include entrance and window backings, ground rows, and the main background in exterior settings. The latter sometimes surrounds the whole acting area and, partly due to its area and to its ability to simulate the sky in all its changes, or to serve as a large canvas on which to paint with light, the means for lighting it constitutes an important item for consideration. Backgrounds should always be subordinate to the main parts of the setting and to the actor. They should aim to carry a suggesion of place and time which stirs the imagination rather than to delineate sharply. The form and painting of the surface, particularly if it is to indicate the middle distance and the far horizon of a landscape in the shallow depth of the stage, must be carefully considered in relation to the available means of lighting it. By changing the lighting it is possible to show the entire course of a day from noon through sunset, midnight, dawn and back to noon again without altering the setting itself in any way. The old painted backdrops with elaborate perspective painting can be lighted by the ordinary borderlights as they

were in the past. But the method for lighting cycloramas here indicated will tend to give much more even
and controlled illumination and a better stage picture
than is possible with backdrops with painted perspective.
Door and window backings should be lighted only
enough so that they do not leave black holes in the setting; to convey the atmosphere of the room or space
beyond. Ground rows always tend to appear flat although they are usually painted to represent rolling
expanses of landscape (*Figure 2, GR*).

CYCLORAMAS

The early back cloths with painted scenes which were
hung to encircle the rear and the two sides of the acting
area were called cycloramas. Although they are seldom
seen now, there are two general types of modern cycloramas, smooth and draped curtains, which follow the
same lines as the old ones but are plain in color; and the
solid quarter sphere called a dome or kuppel-horizont.
The draped curtain cyclorama is nothing more than a
large masking piece taking the place of the wings and
backdrop and usually made of rich material either to
take color well or, like black velvet, to absorb it entirely.
The smooth cyclorama (*Figure 2, C*) is built or hung in
the form of a half-section of a huge cylinder as far from
the acting area as possible to avoid light spill. When used
in this country, the cyclorama is generally painted gray-
blue. In Germany where the stages are generally larger
than ours, two cycloramas that are hung from a curved

track and can be rolled into long vertical cylinders at each side of the stage, are often used. The one is painted white so that it will reflect all colors satisfactorily, the other a dark blue for night skies.

The dome has a floor plan very much like the cyclorama but it curves forward at the top to mask the flies. It is found chiefly where the space over the stage is restricted, and is painted either white or bluish gray. The modern cyclorama or dome is used most often to simulate the vast space of the sky in all its variations.

The chief characteristic of a cloudless sky is its even tone of blue with its variable but carefully blended color changes at the horizon line. The surface of the dome or cyclorama should be free from wrinkles and irregularities and should be lighted so that the unevennesses which are unavoidable are least noticed. The design of settings can be simplified considerably by the use of a properly lighted dome or cyclorama. If, however, there is to be an improvement over the old backdrop which was brightly lighted at the top and bottom and dull in the center, the scenery should be designed to allow for the proper placing of instruments which light the cyclorama.

The lighting of both the dome and the cyclorama is provided by instruments placed at the base and either near the top or at some distance from and above the front of the acting area (*Figure 2, CL*). The instrument at the base generally consists of several sections of relatively high-powered striplights. With the primary colors in these, it is possible to run through all the colors of a sunset. Strips are a great improvement over the large floods (*Figure 20*) often laid on the floor to give this same effect. If the fly space above the stage inside the cyclorama cannot be cleared, a high-powered strip using concentrated reflectors can be mounted near the top of the cyclorama so that its rays are directed down to give an even illumination over the entire surface. This method, however, tends to exaggerate any unevennesses in the surface. The best method for lighting the cyclorama involves the use of a group of floodlights or several sections of directing striplights, hung as far down-stage as possible just out of sight above the acting area to give a fairly direct throw at the large surface.

The total wattage per color circuit for the overhead lights of a cyclorama is, with certain limitations, proportional to the area of the surface lighted. As blue is the predominant color (and lowest in transmission) for these lights it requires more wattage than is necessary for the other colors. If the surface is opaque, less wattage is required than if it is of dyed cloth, and if painted white, less than if gray-blue. In order to produce the effect of a brilliant noonday sky it is wise not to depend upon dense blue mediums but rather to have a circuit of medium steel blues or to mix the two other primary colors with the blue. If the primaries are used they should be of medium density and not as pure as might ordinarily be thought necessary. It is wise to allow for

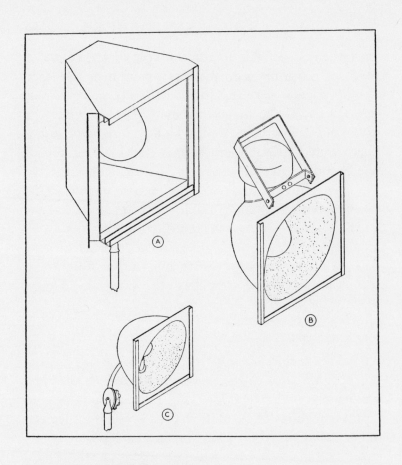

Figure 20: FLOODLIGHTS

 A. Olivette floodlight, using 500-1500 watt pear-shaped lamps, with a flat white or aluminum painted reflector.

 B. Ordinary ellipsoidal floodlight, using either a 500 or 1000 watt pear-shaped lamp.

 C. Small ellipsoidal floodlight using either A-19 100 watt lamp or a 250-400 G-30 spotlight lamp.

the different percentages of transmission of each primary and to adjust the circuit wattages accordingly.

As a basis for the calculation of wattages, 4-8 watts of blue per square foot of surface to be lighted is recommended. Color mediums differ sufficiently to make it impossible to state the relation between the transmission of light by green and red. However, where there are five watts of blue, red will require three watts and green, two. These figures can be multiplied by the number of square feet in the cyclorama area, and then divided by 200, 300, or 500 (the wattage of each lamp) to determine the number of individual units needed for each color. A fourth circuit of white or amber is a practical addition to give a tint of color instead of depending upon the other primaries. In practice all colors are of equal wattage as a rule.

Instruments hung close to the cyclorama should concentrate the rays so that they will project light well up and down the surface to give even illumination.

The overhead lights are assisted in lighting the large surface by the instruments placed at the base. There is considerable leeway here so that the wattages of the overhead and base lights should be considered together. With medium primary color mediums, and efficient concentrating reflectors in the strips laid at the base, about 100-200 watts of blue, 75-150 of red, 60-120 of green and 30-60 watts of white or amber to each running foot of the base of the dome or cyclorama will provide adequate illumination to a height of from eight to fifteen feet. These figures apply to a large cyclorama which has a linear base measurement between 75 and 100 feet. For smaller cycloramas they can be reduced proportionally. The values here given are based on the assumption that length of the cyclorama base strip (horizon strip or cyc foots as it is often called) is never more than 60% of the total length of the base line, not only because the horizon strip follows a shorter radius but also because it is almost never necessary to illuminate the down-stage ends of the cyclorama (*Figure 1, S*). All the wattage must be included within this shorter length but it is figured on the basis of the total base line. If the dome or cyclorama is painted white instead of gray-blue the figures for the overhead and base lights can be cut almost in half, but with a white surface, unless the stage is deep, it is almost impossible to obtain the effect of a midnight sky when the lighting on the acting area is at all bright, due to spill, and reflection from the floor cloth.

In the previous paragraphs it has been indicated that medium red, green, and blue color should be used in both the overhead and the horizon lights. However there are certain limitations to this arrangement. Generally from overhead it may be wise to use only two circuits of blue—two units of medium steel to one of midnight blue. For bright midday the two shades of blue and amber can be used, but for sunset effects the primaries must replace these special colors.

The distribution of light from the overhead instruments should be even, so that the cyclorama surface appears evenly lighted. The light from the horizon strips should blend with the lighting above at an indefinite height and can fall off at the down-stage ends of the cyclorama or dome unless absolute realism is desired. This means that the light must be projected from the best angle that is practical, both from above and below, to give complete color mixing and general, shadowless illumination.

When an ordinary floodlight is placed close to a large surface the fall-off of intensity, as the distance from the instrument increases, is very marked and in order to get an even distribution either the instrument should be placed so that it is equidistant from all parts of the surface, or the reflector must be of such a shape that it can project the rays to the more distant point to equal the illumination on the surface close to the instrument. The beam of light should spread to both sides in a wide angle when the instrument is close to the surface so that rays that come from similarly colored units will mix on the surface close to the instrument. Obviously the horizon strips must be mounted close to the base of the cyclorama in order to leave the acting area free, but as much distance between the strips and the cyclorama as is practical should be allowed. Four feet is many times better than two feet and the smaller the distance the smaller must be the spacing between similar colors in the strip. Sometimes the strip is made in two or three rows to guarantee good color mixing and to get the required wattage in the given space. The same conditions hold for the overhead instruments if they must be mounted close to the cyclorama.

When it is possible to sacrifice the space in the flies for better effect the instruments are hung well down-stage and away from the surface they illuminate. The problem of getting good distribution, color mixing, and eliminating irregularities such as wrinkles and seams which show readily when the light is directed along the surface, is practically solved when the lights are directed at, rather than merely parallel to, the surface of the cyclorama.

The instruments should be medium spread floodlights (*Figure 21*) mounted in several rows over the center of the stage so as to be about equally distant from all parts of the cyclorama, or they may consist of several rows of short strips mounted radially in this same position. With this arrangement a masking border to hide the instruments may be necessary. The height of the border is determined chiefly by the sight line to the top of the cyclorama.

The mounting of the horizon strips is a difficult problem. If they are mounted in a trap or pit there need be no masking ground row. The trap should be broad and deep enough to permit a good color mixing and angle of throw for the strips. This pit should have trap covers

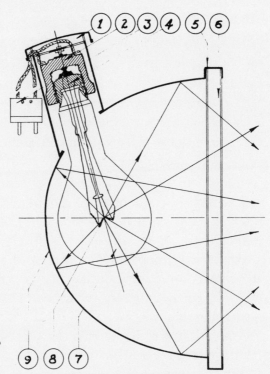

Figure 21:
FLOODLIGHT
SECTION

Section through an ellipsoidal floodlight. The heavy lines with
arrows indicate the direction of the rays of light.

(1) Vent space in cap.
(2) Socket.
(3) Pin connector.
(4) Base of lamp.
(5) Color frame slide cover.
(6) Color frame slide.
(7) Pear-shaped lamp.
(8) Filament.
(9) An ellipsoidal, etched aluminum reflector.

95

which can be closed quickly when the cyclorama is raised for shifting scenery over it. When the strips are set on the floor they should be mounted on trucks equipped with casters so that they can be moved quickly; also a masking ground row is necessary to hide the strips. With fixed domes and cycloramas the pit with portable covers is obviously practical.

The large expanse of a background, such as the cyclorama or dome, presents a tempting opportunity for the technician to "steal the show". Great restraint should govern the tremendous possibilities of distracting the audience by an exciting display of color, form, or movement. Even the intensity of the illumination should be held below the relative values usually given by the sky because, after all, the actor is the point of emphasis in the stage picture. Subtlety of balance in the illumination and in the changes that are included in the course of a scene is the aim of good control.

By using the primary colors, particularly in the horizon strips, a satisfactory range of color simulating the changes of a cloudless sunset can be created. Occasionally just the intensity range of one color is all that is desired. The German apparatus used overhead (*Horizontbeleuchtungsapparat*) is so equipped that the color mediums can be changed over each instrument from the switchboard. This solves the problem of intensity inasmuch as all the instruments can be made to transmit blue or any of five different colors that may be desired. Some

American presentation theatres have adopted the practice of changing color mediums mechanically, because of the increased amount of light that it gives, but at the same time color blending is sacrificed so that this system has its limitations. It is possible to approximate roughly the variety of effects on the horizon which would occur when the sun sets or rises at one side of the stage by controlling the horizon strips in three or more sections, each color in each section being under separate control.

The projection of special effects such as clouds and scenes on the background is considered in another chapter under special instruments, but the German cloud machine which projects moving clouds on the cyclorama is practically a standard piece of equipment in every large European theatre and as such it seems to belong to the background lighting instruments. Actual pictures of clouds are projected in the same manner as with the ordinary lantern slide, and the apparatus is so made that it can revolve and the clouds can be made to cross, to rise or to fall at will. The effect tends to be distracting and will continue to be so until, as with a number of other things of similar nature in the theatre, it becomes commonplace and is accepted. When the background is used as a surface on which to project any definite form it loses its depth and tends to become distracting so that with projected scenery (which some feel is one of the greatest potential contributions of lighting), great care must be taken to keep it a related part of the stage picture.

GROUND ROWS

The most expert painting cannot give ground rows their proper appearance unless the lighting is also well done. It is difficult to give precise directions concerning the lighting of this part of the scenery because so many conditions govern the procedure. However, certain general suggestions can be given which will indicate the right procedure. In the first place the ground row is ordinarily built like a "flat" with an irregular profile edge (*Figure 2, GR*). It is used to represent the middle distances and the horizon and is generally painted to represent rolling hills, mountains, or plains. Often several rows are used to give the sense of greater depth and perspective. They also serve to mask the horizon strips if they are high enough, and they should be designed to allow plenty of space between these strips and the background. A gauze hung in front of the ground row tends to throw it into the distance more than almost anything else. If there are several rows more than one gauze can be used effectively. Generally speaking, if the ground rows can be given some form instead of being flat, it will help to promote plasticity and they will seem less painted. When the overhead lighting for the cyclorama is down-stage, above and in front of the first ground row, this ground row will receive its general lighting from that source, and it will appear as a silhouette when only the horizon lights are used.

Some overhead cyclorama lighting should be provided under most conditions because light from below tends to cast shadows on the background. In front of each ground row, and two feet or more down-stage, it is wise to lay a striplight of one color (generally blue, or three colors if changes are desired) to promote the sense of space between ground rows. Strips thus employed can use 40 watt natural colored lamps because the intensity, unless the ground row is high, should be low. Ordinary backing strips (*Figure 22*) serve this purpose well. Occasionally certain parts of the ground rows such as mountain tops can be picked out, perhaps to show the effect of the setting sun or to give an added accent. In this case a small spotlight carefully matted and directed so that the shadow cast is out of sightline can be used effectively. Any means of giving ground rows more depth and form is an advantage.

BACKINGS

Almost any kind of masking piece that rests on the stage floor is called a backing. It may be a small backdrop representing a high wall when seen through the center door of an interior. It may be a two-leaf screen (the usual form) serving as a door backing to a side entrance, a window backing covered with vines or painted blue to serve as a small sky piece, or an elaborate off-stage room with numerous properties. Broadly, even the wings of the old type of setting might be called backings inasmuch as they set the precedent for lighting this form of background surface. Usually a backing is just a means of concealing the back-stage space that might otherwise be seen by the audience through a door or opening. It certainly should be unobtrusive and it should be lighted so that the opening does not appear as a black hole in the setting. It is practically a rule that all backings must be lighted so that the actor does not seem to make an entrance out of darkness.

There is no necessity to light the actor specially in relation to the backing except at the place where the actor makes an entrance. Strictly speaking the instruments used to light entrances belong to the special group because they usually serve as motivating sources. They must light the actor, and also they are often used to light the background seen through these entrances.

This section deals primarily with the instruments used to light the backings alone or in conjunction with special instruments. The problem is to give a low general distribution over backing surfaces so that they appear to belong to the setting proper. Striplights (*Figure 14*). using the proper colored lamps mounted above or hung at the side of an entrance so that the backing is more or less evenly lighted, and directed so that the actor does not throw a shadow on the backing surface as he enters, can serve this purpose. The strip can consist of from 4-12 (depending upon the size of the opening) 25 to 40 watt lamps of selected color to give the general tone. If it is hung over the door it can be suspended from the back side of the scenery at least three feet above the door itself. If hung vertically it should be at least the same distance down-stage from the door and mounted so that the bottom of the strip is four or five feet from the floor.

Very often it is possible to light a backing with a floodlight of 100 to 500 watts equipped with the proper color and a diffusing medium, or projected through a large diffusing screen. This instrument should always be mounted well above head height and should be so placed that the actor will cast as little shadow as possible. Its position will be close to the setting to get this result. Where color change is necessary more than one floodlight must be used or there must be more than one color circuit in the strip. A window backing can be lighted in much the same manner as is used for any other backing, except that here the movement of actors is generally not involved and the position of the instrument is less crucial. A little experimenting is necessary to determine the best position for the backing light after all the parts of the scenery are in place. Stage braces, which tend to cast shadows, juts in the scenery, and many other unforeseen obstacles, require adjustment. The best instrument is that which gives the most general distribution, and the best position for it is that which is masked from the view of the audience and avoids shadows and the quick drop off in intensity noticed when the instrument is too close to the surface lighted.

CREATING SPECIAL EFFECTS

THE previous chapters have been devoted to the lighting of various parts of the scene that are more or less common to all productions. This chapter deals with the special effects that are often necessary. The layout up to this point guarantees that the acting area will be adequately lighted and that certain broad effects of time of day and composition can be obtained. Like any layout that approaches this degree of standardization it can serve only as a foundation to which the special instruments should be added. It attempts to include equipment that is ordinarily necessary for any type of production, and to limit the variables (which are always too numerous) to such a degree that more attention can be devoted to lighting than to the mechanics of handling instruments. The special effects which must be used to differentiate the lighting of one production from another beyond the variety provided in the basic layout will now be considered.

Although some attempt is made to confine the lighting of the acting space to certain areas it is occasionally necessary to emphasize a particular position on the stage by the use of a special acting area light. Entrances are apt to be more important dramatically than the general acting space, so that it is often desirable to emphasize the actor's face as he enters and leaves the stage. This emphasis must be accomplished with special instruments.

A second group of special instruments is used to serve as motivating sources: to give the effect of sunlight, moonlight, lamplight, firelight, lightning, etc. In realistic settings there is no question concerning the contribution of motivated lighting. In fact, some producers believe that as far as possible all lighting on the stage should be as definitely motivated as the actor's lines and business.

With the less realistic type of play the aim may be expressly to avoid any sense of motivation, but there is a grave question with regard to the ability of the audience to accept any visual effect unless it is motivated to some extent. Our eyes are used to interpret the relation between ourselves and the things about us, so that probably no matter how abstract the setting of a play may be, the audience will supply a motivation for what it sees. Motivation in lighting is more a matter of degree than of sharp delineation but in any case it should create a definite reaction in the audience rather than be neglected because the style of the production is not realistic.

A third group of instruments which create special patterns of light, called "effects", must give a precise control over the form of light even to the extent of giving photographic sharpness of detail. Although the scenic suggestion possible with the motion picture in realistic or totally abstract form, even in color, is available through this type of instrument, its use on the stage is limited, for the present, because it is primarily out of key with the living actor and generally apt to be too distracting to be essentially a dramatic contribution to the production.

EMPHASIS AND ACTING AREA SPECIALS

Particular pieces of scenic detail, special positions within the acting area, and important entrances can be lighted separately to give them added emphasis. As a rule each task of this type requires a separate instrument.

Where some illumination already exists on the object or scenery in question, the additional illumination required to give the necessary emphasis varies with the degree of emphasis desired. Generally this added intensity should not be great because it often appears too arbitrary. The eye can easily perceive a difference of intensity between different areas if the difference is greater than one-tenth of the existing illumination. If one foot-candle exists, one-tenth may be added to give emphasis. If ten foot-candles are incident on a surface one foot-candle added to an object will make it seem to stand out. Inasmuch as the special illumination must be confined to a certain area it is wise to use a lens unit to get the desired control. The added intensity that is given by having the lamp at relatively sharp focus indicates that the special instrument can be of lower wattage than the lens unit generally used at the same distance for acting area lighting.

In accenting a part of the scenic detail such as a tapestry or picture, color is important. It is best to select a tint similar to the dominant color of the pigment, but the special illumination must not differ too much from the general color on the adjacent parts of the setting.

The beam of light should be shaped to correspond to the outlines of the object lighted or soft edged so that it fades into the surrounding lighting. The beam from a lens unit can be shaped by an opaque mat cut to the desired shape and mounted in the color frame (*Figure 11*). For precise patterns an objective system such as is used in the effect machine must be used because an ordinary spotlight will give a "fuzzy" edge. The instrument, usually mounted behind the teaser so that the beam will not have to be directed through the acting area where shadows of the actors would be cast on the object, should have a position which directs the beam most squarely at the object. Distortion due to a diagonal throw must be allowed for in making the mat. It is important to have this special instrument under the control of a dimmer or to select the color medium of the requisite density so that the intensity of illumination of a particular area can be balanced with that of the surrounding areas.

Special positions within the general acting areas, particularly those which fall between two of the conventional areas or in an inaccessible corner of the setting must be lighted as essential parts of the acting area. The illumination of those special areas where important pieces of business may transpire during the course of the scene is, in present professional practice, about the only use to which acting area spotlights are put. The borders and foots are expected to illuminate those areas which are not specially spotted. Obviously such a practice requires many special instruments or a great deal of refocusing between scenes to make the instruments direct their beams on a different set of areas for each scene. With the method suggested for lighting the six conventional areas, or as many as seem necessary, the number of special instruments can be cut down to the minimum.

The amount of illumination given by special acting area spotlights should be consistent with the intensity given to the other areas and can be figured from the tables given on page 35. Where accent is to be given within one of the conventional areas the suggestions in the previous paragraph hold. The color should be consistent with the other acting areas or selected to give the special effect desired. The area to be lighted determines the shape of the beam and the position for mounting the instrument. Generally the beam should be soft edged but where there is already considerable illumination the shape of the beam is not likely to show. Quite often the special areas require illumination from both sides and equally as often the area is so surrounded by scenery that the ground plans and drawings should be studied with great care to provide for placing special instruments where they can be most effective.

For special distributions and directions such as the effect of light from a fireplace or from a trap in the floor the placing of the instrument depends considerably upon the position where the shadow of the actor will fall. Where a broad spread of light from special positions is desired a floodlight is ordinarily more efficient than a lens unit. Usually, however, a spotlight mounted in the proper position behind the teaser or in a ceiling beam will give the best results. If it is necessary to have a color change within an area another instrument will have to be used in addition to the one already covering the area. By dimming one instrument and bringing up the other the form of light is not changed but the color is.

In repertory theatres it is thought more efficient to use two or three spotlights in place of each acting area spot in the conventional system suggested in the second chapter, to provide the color change from scene to scene. This system saves labor, but color change can be accomplished equally well by the use of remotely controlled boomerangs which will allow at least four different color changes for each instrument and are under control from the switchboard. When soft-edged follow spots, controlled in direction from the switchboard, are developed, and the toning and blending lighting handled so that the proper distribution is given over the acting area, it may be possible to eliminate most of the complication of the general acting area spotlighting. The problem then will be the training of the operator to follow each actor, perhaps from two sides, as he moves about the stage. This may take a long time and may never be realized but it is an interesting speculation. Follow spots as we know them today belong essentially to the musical or stylized types of production. An easy method to use for following under some conditions is to mount a mirror on a universal joint in front of the spotlight, and to direct the beam by moving the mirror and not the spotlight itself.

Entrance lighting originated in the days when entrances could be made between the wings. The wing strips illuminated the actor as he came on and left the stage. Later when floodlights were developed it became the practice to place a flood in each wing or entrance and to some extent the effect that this practice gave is necessary even today. Backing lights as we know them should not be expected to perform the function of entrance illumination. Conversely, however, the entrance lights are often supposed to light the backings as well as the actor as he enters or leaves the set.

There is another type of entrance light which is essentially a special acting area instrument. This instrument, a lens unit, is generally equipped with a mat to shape the beam to fit the door opening or entrance. It is used primarily to accent the actor as he makes his entrance to the acting space. Its color and intensity are generally that of the other acting area lights and it is generally mounted behind the teaser so that the throw of the beam is as direct as possible. An instrument directed through the entrance from off-stage may be of the same type if no spill on the backing is wanted, but generally the off-stage instrument is a floodlight mounted well above the actor's head and some distance away from the entrance to keep the actor's shadow from falling on the backing or into the set itself. If this instrument is thoroughly diffused the shadow made when its beam is intercepted will be soft edged, and the illumination can serve as the general light filling the off-stage room.

There are two devices for obtaining diffusion which are better than a diffusing medium. One is to project the light through a large translucent screen, and the other is to direct a high-powered spotlight from a high angle beyond the off-stage edge of the backing to a large white diffusing surface placed parallel to the backing on the down-stage side of the opening.

The color to use in entrance lighting instruments, unless it serves as the motivating light of the sun or some other source, can be complementary in color to the general lighting on the stage. The intensity must naturally be low so that the entrance does not appear distracting. As a general rule, if an actor approaches an entrance in the rear wall of the setting from both sides of the stage, there should be floodlights or spotlights placed on each side. When the actor is making an exit or entrance these special instruments as well as the acting area lights of the playing space will light him.

MOTIVATING LIGHT

All lighting should be dramatic, a component part of the means of expression in a production. It should be convincing and not distracting. But our sensibilities have become so dulled by seeing the conventional that we are prone to lose track of the real. The suggestions for lighting made in the first chapters of this plan are primarily practical; they constitute an arbitrary means of creating the visual aspect of a scene; they are in a measure unmotivated, undramatic. This section is devoted to the discussion of light sources which may be called realistic, but the intention is not to define the bounds of realism, but to give practical examples of a larger field of expression.

It is almost too much to expect that a slice of nature set upon the stage would be dramatic even if it were possible to reproduce it with photographic accuracy. And it is only rarely possible, through careful direction and design, to make the motivating source give all the illumination that is necessary. In any case a scene is apt to be more convincing if sunlight streaming in at the window, or a table lamp set beside a chair, illuminate it naturally, as far as possible, without giving a glare to the eyes of the audience. Therefore, the technician must resort to auxiliary sources, such as acting area and emphasis lights to supplement the motivating sources. The effect of the combination is motivated lighting.

Sunlight

It is possible to justify the lighting of a daytime scene by directing the bright warm rays of the sun into the acting area or on some essential piece of scenery. Light thus used can serve as part of the acting area lighting and will tend to motivate the brighter illumination of the whole acting area even if it falls on only a portion of the stage or through a window in an interior. It should be bright, the brightest light on the stage, somewhere between 10 and 100 foot-candles depending upon the time of day and the general brightness over the rest of the stage. It approximates the brightness of the sunlight entering the window of a room as compared to the brightness inside. Its color should be warm, but not the particular greenish yellow shade resulting from the wrong use of a straw medium. The uncolored light from an incandescent lamp (particularly if the lamp is dimmed slightly) will appear warm if the rest of the stage is bathed in the cool tints of daylight. Amber of varying grades will give the range of color needed to indicate sunset. Whenever possible the direction of the rays should be such that they tend to illuminate the face of the actor on the side toward the audience. The angle of the beam of light is obviously determined by the time of day and the rays should be *parallel*. There is only one instrument which could even approximate this effect over the whole stage, and then only if it could be mounted at a great distance from the stage. This is a high-powered searchlight. It is possible, however, to use smaller instruments closer to the stage if they are limited to lighting a small area only. When a large area must be lighted, several instruments properly spaced and focused in the same general direction can be used with relatively satisfactory results. Generally speaking, a "sunspot" is used and the acting area lights directed from that side are equipped with a similar color. The conventional instrument for simulating sunlight is the open floodlight, or Olivette (*Figure 20A*). It is very poorly suited to this purpose. When placed just outside a window or entrance so that its rays spread in a wide beam into the room, it does not cast the same parallel rays or cause the same shadows as the sun, nor does its intensity carry from one side of the stage to the other.

To simulate sunlight correctly, some type of concentrating instrument must be mounted as far from the stage as possible and as high as is consistent with the angle of the rays. This is often very difficult since designers seldom consider the possible locations for "sunspots" with respect to the position and shape of the windows they put in their settings. With poorly designed sets, incorrect motivation for the lighting is not always the electrician's fault. The types of instruments best suited for the purpose of simulating sunlight are the projector (*Figures 22 and 23*) and the high-powered spotlight. Due to the fact that the reflector gathers more rays than the lens of a plano-convex spotlight, the pro-

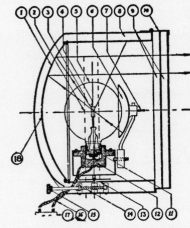

Figure 22:
PROJECTOR—
SHALLOW REFLECTOR
*Section of an open-faced pro-
jector. The rays that would
normally come out the front of
the hood are redirected by a
spherical mirror. It is not ordinarily as efficient as the type
illustrated in 24. Heavy lines
with arrows indicate direction
of rays of light.*

(*1*) Large parabolic reflector.

(*2*) The flood focal position.

(*3*) A concentrated high-powered filament, preferably monoplane type.

(*4*) The sharp focus position, or focal centre of the reflector.

(*5*) Bulb of the G-type lamp.

(*6*) Spherical reflector, mounted on the lamp carriage so that
it lies on the axis of the parabolic reflector and its centre
of curvature lies at the centre of the filament.

(*7*) Reflector adjustment.

(*8*) Ventilation space.

(*9*) Color frame slides.

(*10*) Color frame slide closer to prevent light spill.

(*11*) Base of the lamp. (*12*) Socket.

(*13*) Focal slide. (*14*) Worm focal adjustment.

(*15*) Focal adjustment knob.

(*16*) Asbestos insulated feeds.

(*17*) Pin connector. (*18*) Vent hole.

jector is from three to six times as efficient in terms of intensity as the conventional spotlight. It is far less flexible in control, however, and more clumsy than the spotlight, so that the large step lens unit is probably the best to use. The spread of the beam from the projector is limited, it cannot be shielded except by an extremely long funnel, and the beam is very apt to be mottled. This last characteristic can be somewhat counteracted by the use of a color medium, and the mottling often gives a very desirable variety that can be obtained in the beam cast by a spotlight only by using a variegated gelatin.

Often the acting area spotlights from one side can be used to give the effect of sunlight without using special instruments. The changes in brightness can be controlled at the switchboard by the dimmers. Sometimes it is wise to use more than one sunlight instrument if a change in color and direction is required. A color boomerang which allows the movement of increasingly deep amber mediums over the face of the instrument, and a stand with a windlass which permits the lowering of the instrument and the changing of the direction of the rays, can be used for the same purpose.

Moonlight

About the only difference between sunlight and moonlight on the stage is the intensity and color. The same instruments may be used for both, and the same rules govern their use. The intensity of moonlight in nature is ordinarily far too weak to provide adequate visibility lighting so that it is stage practice to "steal" considerably on the side of brightness. Generally the same wattage as that used for sunlight must be used in the instruments simulating moonlight because of the increased need of intensity and because the blue medium transmits less than a third of the amount of light that is passed by the amber. The actual color of moonlight is an indescribable greenish-blue which is not complimentary to the make-up. Most equipment companies sell a special moonlight color which approximates the true color, but a deep steel-blue (or light purple-blue) is not far from the actual color and it is less hard on the make-up than any other shade of blue. If this color is used in the acting area spotlights from one side to serve as the motivating light, the spotlights on the other side of the stage can use light blue or a medium blue at lower intensity than the moonlight.

Daylight

Daylight is the general cool light coming in all directions from the sky. The toning and blending instruments used alone can produce this effect approximately, but acting area lights and other special instruments must be used to give the proper visibility. Daylight is given by such a broad general source that it is absolutely shadowless, so that any directional light which tends to produce shadows is not apt to be convincing as daylight.

The intensity of daylight is easy to simulate. In nature it ranges between a fraction of a foot-candle to several thousand, depending upon the position of the sun and the presence of clouds, but as little as ten foot-candles of general illumination on the stage conveys the impression adequately.

The color of daylight when approximated by incandescent sources can be obtained by the use of a color medium of a light steel blue which verges on purple.

The general shadowless distribution is difficult to obtain. Any means that will eliminate or reduce shadows or have them fall where they are not noticed will aid in giving the effect. Daylight entering a window can be simulated by the use of a large reflecting screen or several small floods equipped with the steel and diffusing mediums. Striplights tend to give the most shadowless illumination, but daylight seems to have more penetrating power than they provide. This is illustrated by the attempts to light windows artificially. The illuminated white reflecting surface seen through the window may be bright, even approaching a glare, but the amount of light that gets into the room does not compare with the daylight given by nature, and the sky certainly seldom seems to glare.

Changes in daylight coloring from dawn through sunset are very subtle and probably can best be provided by the progressive addition of circuits of light green-blue and violet to the steel. The general light of an extremely hot day may require white or even light amber to emphasize the atmosphere. The light given by a cloudy sky is almost colorless.

Fixture Lighting

A room lighted by stand lamps and wall brackets is seldom lighted brightly enough for visibility on the stage. Moreover, in such a room, the light sources would appear glaring to the audience sitting in the darkened auditorium even though well shielded and of very low wattage. The habit of avoiding bright lights where they fall on the face and in the line of vision is growing. The actor must be a brazen individual to seek the spotlight against all sense of comfort, but he knows that unless he is looking into a glaring light, his face is probably not sufficiently visible to make his facial expression clear; without it he is robbed of one of his chief tools of expression. The lighting designer soon learns to love the actor who seeks the spotlight, because the novice is constantly seeking the shadows, or at least seldom knows that he can be seen best where he can see a light source—the brighter the better.

Fixtures on the stage are essentially decorative and when lighted serve primarily as motivating sources. They should never, in contrast to actual conditions, be bright enough (on the side toward the audience) to seem glaring in the stage picture. However, if they are well shielded, they can house large enough lamps to give considerable illumination. Then the effect of the rest of the lighting, if carefully balanced, will seem justified and natural.

A completely realistic use of fixture lighting on the stage would not be in harmony with other methods of lighting nor would it usually give adequate illumination. The audience expects something in addition to photographic realism, so that no great effort ought to be made to have all the lighting come from fixtures unless they thereby contribute something dramatic. It is easier to create an effect by using normal acting area and tonal lighting and making the illumination seem to come from the fixture. Perhaps as long as fixtures are present it may be well to try to design them so that they can give some of the illumination necessary.

It is better to light the stage by the normal method from hidden sources than to have "hot spots" in the line of vision, or to load the stage with special instruments that "spot" the areas ordinarily lighted by the fixture. Common practice involves the use of many special instruments in the manner just cited. The effects resulting from the practice are often crude, easily discernible and therefore less effective than are those resulting from lighting by acting area and tonal lights. Unless the fixture can be made to give some illumination, it should be decorative only and serve as a simulating, motivating source.

Fixtures can be divided into two groups: those which are only decorative and those which, in addition, give illumination. The intensity of the first group is directly dependent upon the reflecting power and illumination of the scenery against which they are to be seen. If the lamp itself is to be seen, the true size should be used, but it should be dimmed so that it does not seem "hot" against the background. It should be just bright enough to serve as a suitable accent in the stage picture. Unless there are a number of these lamps used together on the stage so that the total wattage will equal that of the dimmer controlling them, it is necessary to provide a special small dimmer or, more practically, to connect sufficient wattage (off-stage) to the same dimmer so that it will be properly loaded. This off-stage resistance is called a "ghost" or "phantom" load.

Another method of reducing the intensity of light from visible lamps is to frost each one so that it transmits no more light than is necessary for the particular position in which it is used. This assumes that the several lamps, which may be used about the set and connected to the same dimmer, must be of different intensities in conformity with their surroundings. Wherever possible the lamp should be covered with a shade. From 10 to 25 watts will give the necessary glow on the adjacent wall or surface.

The shaded fixture can be made to give some illumination, either by dipping the lamp a dark color on the side facing the audience or by making the shade more dense on that side. In some cases the up-stage side of the shade can be cut away to allow direct emanation from the lamp to fall on the acting area and the scenery behind the fixture. Obviously, in this case a lamp as large as the fixture can accommodate should be used. If the fixture is to be the chief source of illumination it must be specially designed to carry the proper lamp, to accommodate reflectors and even lenses to direct the light, and still to appear in character with its surroundings. The color of the light should be similar to that expected by the audience unless a special effect is desired.

Central ceiling fixtures are generally hung from a special line, independent of those supporting the ceiling and so that they can be let down to the floor and unhooked when the scene is struck. Under no conditions should the weight of the fixture be supported by the feed cable. The cable is usually attached to the supporting line and taken out of the way with it when the set is struck. This means that there should be a connector at the instrument. A large inverted cup called the canopy at the top of the fixture where it meets the ceiling will conceal the connectors and the hook of the supporting line.

Wall brackets should have the same wattage and construction as ceiling fixtures, except that they are hung from the scenery itself as a rule. Table lamps and stand lamps generally have long enough stage cable leads to reach to the nearest up-stage or off-stage part of the scenery where the leads are passed through small holes and connected to their feed cables.

Where there is danger that the run of cable across the floor will be kicked or tripped over, the cable should be tied to the leg of the table or stand and covered with a rug if possible. Only on rare occasions should the actor be required to turn the switch which lights a fixture. The control should be kept at the switchboard as far as possible and a cue signalled from a vantage point. In lighting a fixture the actor should not throw the switch but should keep his hand on it until the light comes on.

Lamplight

It is always safer to use an electric source simulating the flame than the actual oil and wick. A small candelabra lamp fed by the regular current can be used if the lamp is not carried on stage. If it must be brought into the room, lighted, a battery can be built into the oil container and a flashlight lamp used as the source. Under some conditions a portable lamp can be brought in unlighted and connected after it is put in place. The lamp can be dipped or covered with gelatin of a light amber shade. The lamp chimney should be frosted or smoked on the audience side so that the source does not glare or reveal its static nature and false shape. If it is necessary to light the lamp the actor should cover the business as naturally as possible and the light should be brought up from the switchboard on cue with the auxiliary lighting which the lamp should seem to motivate. The battery type of lamp can have a small dimmer mounted on the fixture itself or, if the business is covered by the actor, can be snapped on by means of a switch.

Candlelight

Many of the suggestions made in the paragraph on lamplight hold for candlelight, but with special permission from the Fire Inspector in most cities, real candles can be used on stage, provided they are substantially mounted and are not used close to the scenery. Some cities require the use of a mica lamp chimney around each candle. The effect is definitely artificial. The flame shaped lamps made by the lamp companies do not simulate candles successfully unless they are to be seen at a great distance. There is a product which has a small filament in a flame shaped parchment and a resistance in the body of the candle that gives quite a natural shape to an electric source. Small battery lamps covered with a twisted piece of amber and frost gelatin will give a good shape to the electric source.

But nothing can simulate the flickering quality of the real candle. When the real or artificial source is used exposed and the rest of the stage is dark, even one candle will seem to glare. If the candle must be exposed, the rest of the stage should be bright enough to offset this glare; when shielded, a small electric lamp will give more illumination and be more satisfactory than the actual candle except for the flicker which, after all, is apt to be more distracting than contributing. As mentioned before, the auxiliary lighting should be carefully balanced to keep from seeming artificial. A single spotlight directed on the area supposed to be lighted by the candle should be soft-edged and accompanied by low general illumination of the proper distribution and color.

Torchlight

Nothing can be more ridiculous than the average stage torch. It is often wiser to do without it than to try to simulate torchlight. A long stick with a battery and lamp on the end, perhaps covered with flame shaped gelatin or tissue, is the usual stock device for simulating the torch, and unless seen from some distance, it is unconvincing indeed. A large torch of the brazier form, particularly if it is not portable, can house a lamp large enough to give some light and in a more elaborate form can have a number of short silk pennants which are blown upward by a small electric fan. The lamp should be amber in color. The torchlight should be supported by other lighting because it can give very little illumination itself. A soft-edged, warm light coming from the general direction of the motivating light will produce approximately the right effect. When the torch itself is not seen, the effect of torchlight can be given by a floodlight placed where the torch would be, and if the flicker is important, silk banners agitated over the face of the flood by a fan or an out-of-focus fire "effect" can be used.

Firelight

The dramatic nature of fire makes it an important feature of expression in theatrical production. It is more a type of "effect" than a motivating source, as a rule, but is treated here inasmuch as it occasionally serves the dual purpose. The producer may expect a script to call for any form of fire from the ambitious demands of Wagner's *Valkyrie* where flame and smoke engulf the stage, to the modest glow of a coal-grate.

Coal-grates give very little lighting effect in the room unless flames or a very low glow are desired. Flames can be simulated in the manner suggested for torches, but the banners can be longer and there can be several rows of them. The glowing coal can be amber dipped glass pieces (broken lenses), partially blackened with paint. If this is packed around a wire screen box, covered with amber and red variegated gelatin, and in which two *rotors* are mounted, the moving light effect associated with heat and flames will be cast about the room and particularly on the fireplace backing. The two rotors are painted transparent cylinders, with light metal-vaned tops, which are mounted on the top of a lamp so that they turn freely in opposite directions, due to the up-draught of the heated air from the lamp (perhaps 100 to 250 watts). Diagonal streaks of red and amber with a certain amount of black will give the desired flicker. The rotors should turn freely on glass bearings. The speed can be controlled by the pitch of the vanes. The effect in the room can be increased for visibility sake by installing a baby spotlight or flood (250 to 400 watts) out of sight at the side of the fire grate, and its effect can be varied on dimmers or by means of a fan and silk banners, but this last means is not particularly desirable because of its distracting effect.

Fire logs should be made hollow to house small amber and red lamps. The flame, if desired, can be made as suggested above. If the part that is to glow is left translucent when the logs are painted, the red glow will seem to come from the fire itself. The ash heap can even contain two rotors, if there is space. Smoke can be made by chemical means. The effect of the fire's glowing and changing can be accomplished by dimming separately the various lamps used inside the logs.

Open fires such as campfires can be made in the same fashion as the fire logs just described. A simple method is to use actual sticks and logs and to build them into a pyramid over a small lamp covered with red or amber gelatin. Chemical smoke does not tend to rise very rapidly so that if the fire is a large one which involves the use of smoke, steam should be piped under the stage to this point. The great drawback to the use of steam is the noise it makes if allowed to escape under high pressure. Smoke pots that are used in fireworks displays have sometimes been used on the stage, but the heavy fumes that accompany the smoke are apt to float out into the auditorium and annoy the audience.

Conflagrations had better be kept off-stage and only their effect shown. In the *Valkyrie* the flames have been simulated by placing long steam pipes drilled with many holes behind ground rows and throwing amber color from striplights on the steam as it rises. To show the effect of a fire close by, an out-of-focus fire "effect" placed offstage can give the flicker and color desired. For distant fires a dull red glow from an off-stage floodlight is sufficient to suggest what is happening.

"EFFECTS"

Under this heading come the patterns of light that do not, as a rule, serve to illuminate as much as to create recognizable forms such as clouds, lightning, and rain. There are two general types of instruments in this class; the Linnebach lantern and the effect machine. With these instruments many astounding effects of lighting, that were the wonder of the theatre a generation ago and are still used extensively for novelty purposes, can be produced with relative ease. However, lighting that pretends to be subtle and a contributing factor to the dramatic action of the play must employ lighting "effects" with great care and reserve, particularly moving projections. The instruments that project "effects" can contribute so much to please the eye that the temptation to overuse must be carefully suppressed. Simple as these machines are in themselves, there is almost no end to the experimentation necessary to make them effective dramatically. Distortion of the projected image, "paintiness", distracting brightness, difficulty in operation, and the vividness of projected patterns compared to those that are painted, present problems that can be solved for each attempt only by experience. No effect can be satisfactory if it is not considered in the design of a particular setting and often in the directing of the play.

The Linnebach Lantern

The Linnebach lantern (*Figure 23*) operates on the principle of shadow projection. A small high-powered light source, such as a concentrated filament, or, better still an arc, sends its rays directly through a large painted glass or gelatin slide and projects the pattern on a large screen. The size of the slide, its relation to the light source and the distance between the instrument and the screen determine the size of the image. Anyone knows that as he approaches a light source his shadow increases in size and the edges become more blurred. If a flat object is held upright parallel to the wall a large shadow will be cast, and it will have the same proportions as the object itself. If the object is tipped the shadow shows a distorted form; not the true shape of the object. This is one of the greatest problems which must be dealt with in projecting patterns because it is not often that a direct throw to the screen can be obtained. If the slide can be placed parallel to the screen the distortion will be eliminated. In case it cannot, by trial and error a specially squared slide which allows for the distortion can be made and the distortion can be corrected on the slide itself. The slide is mounted at the front of a large tapered black funnel with the light source at the small end, as far from the slide as possible, so that the image will be sharp. The size of the front of the funnel de-

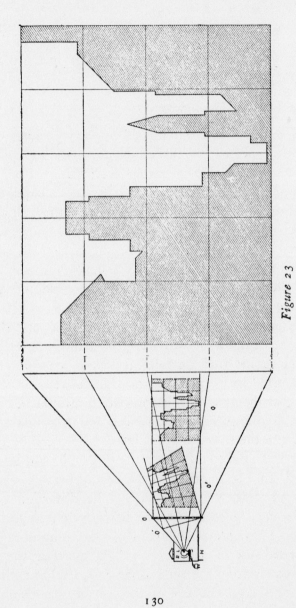

Figure 23

termines the size of the image at each distance from the screen. The spread of the funnel should be from 60° to 90°.

This instrument can be used to project a bold colored pattern over a large surface at close range. The pattern must be bold because the size of a light source will always blur the edges somewhat, and it should be used close to the screen because its intensity when spread over a large area will always be low. Color when projected in this manner will appear very brilliant or painty unless it is carefully handled because of the contrast with the dark areas that accompany it. It goes without saying that there should be very little other light on the screen if the projection is to count.

Figure 23: LINNEBACH LANTERN

A. Linnebach lantern or projector, showing two slides for producing the same image.

O and O'. Plate glass on which the scene is painted. O' slanted, O parallel to the screen. When the slide is parallel to the screen, the image is not distorted. The fine lines indicate the plotted squares which serve as a guide in the construction of the slide. O' shows the construction of the slide when it is used at an angle to the screen.

H. The hood which is painted dead black inside.

R. Reflector.

L. Light source, which is a high-powered concentrated filament lamp or an arc source (in the latter case, the reflector is not used).

S. Screen. Translucent if the projection is from behind, white if from the front.

The position of the instrument is usually behind a translucent screen because of the lack of space in front. If this screen is semi-transparent, the instrument should be placed on the floor. A masking screen put between it and the sightlines of the audience will eliminate the possibility of seeing the light source through it. When the instrument is placed on the floor the drop of intensity due to the increased distance to the top of the screen will be very marked. If the instrument can be mounted in front of the screen much greater brilliance can be obtained. When an arc is used there is apt to be a distracting flicker, but a much sharper and brighter image than is possible with an incandescent light source will result. However, with the incandescent lamp, by using two instruments placed side by side, it is possible to fade from one pattern to the next. If the slides are painted to represent a scene that might be painted on a backdrop, the scene can be made to change before the eyes of the audience by dimming one unit and bringing up the other. The effect will never be as clear cut as a painted scene, but it will be much more vivid—often too bright.

The Effect Machine

The Effect Machine (*Figure 24*) is similar in its principle of operation to the old magic lantern or the modern lantern slide projector. An extra condensing lens called a "dutchman", a slide, and an objective lens are

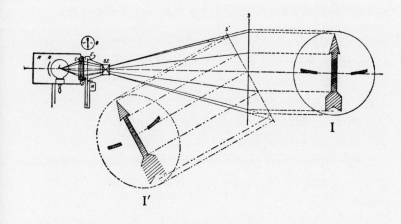

Figure 24: THE EFFECT MACHINE

I shows normal direct projection similar to the lantern slide or stereopticon. I' shows the distortion due to angular projection.

The space between the cross-hatching indicates the relative intensity of the rays of the various parts of the image, and in the case of I', they are supposed to indicate the blurring of the edges of the image at the extremes, assuming that the centre is in focus.

H. Hood.

R. Spherical reflector.

L. Concentrated light source. An arc if the throw is long or a bright image is desired.

C. Condensing lens.

D. Extra-condensing lens or dutchman.

E. The effect drum.

M. Clock-work drive or electric motor.

O. The object painted on the effect drum.

O.S. The objective system, consisting of two small lenses.

S and S'. The screen.

I and I'. The image.

added to the front of a standard plano-convex lens spot-light to make the instrument called an effect machine. The effect machine is used primarily to project precise images on a large screen which forms part of the setting. It differs in effect from the Linnebach lantern in that its image is sharper, less intense, and smaller. It requires a longer throw and the slide must be made with photographic precision because every detail is magnified many times.

The instrument is less bulky and can be equipped with moving slides more easily than the shadow projector. It is subject to the same problem of distortion to an even greater degree and it requires almost a direct throw if the image is to be in focus over all its area. Another specific feature that complicates the use of the effect machine is that there is a direct relation between the size of the slide, the size of the image, and the focal length of the objective lens. The intensity of the effect machine is so low that the largest size of the slide which any given machine will accommodate must ordinarily be used; seldom larger than a four inch circle or a rectangle contained within this circle. The relationship of the variables can be stated in the following formulas:

$$(1)* \quad \frac{p}{P} = \frac{q}{Q} \qquad and \qquad (2) \quad \frac{1}{p} + \frac{1}{q} = \frac{1}{f}$$

Example: It is desired to project a $10'$ image at $20'$ from a $3''$ slide.

(1) $\frac{p}{3} = \frac{20'}{10'}$, $p = 6''$, so that (2) $\frac{1}{6} + \frac{1}{240} = \frac{1}{f}$, $f = 5.75''$

$5''$ is the next shortest and the nearest practical "f."

where p is the distance from the slide to the optical center of the objective lens system, q is the distance from the instrument to the screen; f is the focal length of the objective lens system; P is the size or diameter of the slide and Q is the size or diameter of the image. Equipment companies are in the habit of rating their short focal length objectives according to the focal length of each of the two lenses in the objective so that in effect the focal length is about one-half its rated figure.

It is possible to fabricate special focal length objectives by using two different focal length lenses, or to give a certain range of focal length to one combination by varying the distance between the lenses in the objective. The resultant focal length for each case can be determined by the following formula:

$$(3)* \quad f = \frac{f_1 \times f_2}{f_1 + f_2 - d}$$

where f is the focal length of the combination, the lenses a certain distance apart d, and f_1 is the focal length of the first lens and f_2 that of the second.

The formulas are included here only to show the variables involved and their relation to each other. Equipment firms generally list the range of image size

---

Example: A 5" focal length objective using 8" and 10" lenses to make the combination. How far apart should they be?

$$5 = \frac{8 \times 10}{8 + 10 - d}, \quad d = 2".$$

If d is fixed due to the size of the holder then it is a matter of cut and try. And an 8 and a 12 at 2" apart $= \dfrac{8 \times 12}{8 + 12 - 2} = 5.33"$

given by each focal length objective at different distances assuming the object to be a 4½″ circle or a standard 3¼ x 4″ slide. If the image is too large either a longer focal length lens must be used or the slide must be made smaller by means of a framing cutoff. The range of focus for each set of conditions is relatively limited so that a diagonal throw to the screen will not only distort the image but will tend to give a blurred effect on the parts of the screen nearest and farthest from the instrument if the center is "in focus". The distortion can be allowed for in making the slide, but there is practically no method of bringing all parts of the image in sharp focus when the angle of throw is sharp.

While the effect machine is most often used to produce sharp images, occasionally a soft effect is more in keeping than a sharp one. This can be accomplished by moving the objective lens to "out of focus" position. Another factor that makes the formulas important is the limitation of positions for both the screen and the instrument. The design of the setting almost always determines the size of the image and thereby indirectly establishes or limits closely the positions of the instrument and the screen. With the positions and therefore the distance between instrument and screen established, and the desirability of using as large a slide as possible for the sake of intensity, the only variable that remains to be determined is the focal length of the objective.

The lens of a spotlight intercepts so small a portion of the light created at the source that the greatest efficiency of this instrument is seldom over ten per cent. If the dutchman and the lenses in the objective each eliminate ten per cent of this small amount of light, in addition to that lost in transmission through the slide, it will be clear that an effect machine must either have a large light source or the image will be of low brightness. For a moderately dim stage, an average size of image, and a good reflecting screen, a 2000 watt lamp will give a fair brightness up to a 20′ throw. Beyond that distance a 5000 watt spotlight or an arc must be used. The colors used in making the slide should be very transparent. It is difficult to color a projection slide by hand because every detail is enlarged many times in the image. A very carefully taken, natural color photograph of a large sketch would come close to being the ideal projection slide. The same limitations apply to the forms and details of the slide. There is a German firm which makes a large model of a scene and then photographs it from the same relative position that the effect machine will have on the stage. In this way slides which register distortion and color with photographic accuracy can be made.

The effect machine provides a simple method of covering large surfaces with a precise pattern. The number of effects that can be made is of course unlimited, particularly when several effect machines are used simultaneously. No attempt is made here to describe in detail how most effects are made because a little ingenuity will answer this question provided that the general principle is understood. Though most projections have a limited effectiveness they are amusing to deal with. In general it is wise to rent the more complicated slides, or "effects", as they are called. They are likely to be expensive, but they are more carefully prepared than the home-made product. This advice applies particularly to the so-called "moving effect" which usually consists of a large round metal drum with one or more painted mica discs. The disc is rotated by a clock-works or a small electric motor which can be controlled from the switchboard. The German cloud machine consists of several individual effect machines with photographs of clouds which are rotated about one central high-powered source. Moving effects except rain, snow, fire, water ripple, and perhaps moving clouds should be willingly dedicated to the revue and musical comedy stage where novelty is a virtue. It need hardly be mentioned that the stationary slide, like the lantern slide, is placed in the machine upside down and that moving effects will give the image a movement in the opposite direction from that in which the disc is turning.

The rain effect is convincing when projected on a front gauze or a large backdrop and the rest of the stage kept in relative darkness. The disc is painted dead black and minute needle scratches, made in irregular parallel lengths, show as a downpour of rain.

Stars can be projected over a small area by the use of a long focal length lens. A thin opaque card pricked by very fine points in a slight variety of size and spacing will give this effect, but the area must be very small; otherwise the stars will look as large as snowballs. A blue color medium should be used.

With a fine pointed stylus a bolt of lightning can be scratched out, preferably copied from a picture, on a lamp-blacked plate of glass. If a slotted shutter is mounted in the slide carrier with the slide, the effect of a streak of lightning can be given by passing the slot quickly from the bottom to the top of the slide. The shutter must be at the slide position because no other place is in focus and the cutoff can only be sharp at that point.

Snow effects are similar to rain except that the scratches are shorter and farther apart. Also the drum is rotated at a slower speed.

Clouds, unless they are photographed or thrown out of focus, are apt to appear crude. Photographs taken and developed to give sharp contrast are best for this purpose. The sky part of the picture should be blocked out. Moving cloud discs are generally painted by hand and are only really effective as storm clouds. A good approximation of lightning flashing between clouds can be given if a storm cloud effect is flashed on the background from time to time.

Fire effects can be projected fairly successfully over a small area by revolving two or three painted discs at different speeds in the same drum. Each slide should be painted so that the movement within the movement makes the painted forms seem to turn and rise.

The water ripple consists of several moving parts made of ripple-glass. A piece of flat glass painted with horizontal lines of blue and green alternated with clear spaces between can be moved up and down slowly to produce the ripple movement. If an irregular mat shaped like the path of light from the moon on the water is placed in the slide, the soft ripple of the path of moonbeams on water can be simulated. A color medium of blue-green may be necessary to give the proper color.

A hasty survey of the lists in various catalogues will reveal a host of other effects, but those here listed are most generally useful on the legitimate stage and are designed to give realistic patterns. The effect machine will be of relatively little use, however, until the principle of projection is extended into the more abstract type of design. It is far more suitable in the latter field because its effect is always somewhat distorted and conventionalized. A vast store of visual expression awaits the designer who can incorporate the compelling visual reaction to changing light patterns over the great expanse of the stage, into a co-ordinated dramatic expression as carefully executed as are the more limited means of expression he is using today.

OTHER USES OF LIGHT

There are certain other uses of light that cannot strictly be called "effects" (definite patterns of light), but that have an important place in any discussion of lighting methods.

Luminescence is the special effect given by some chemicals due to their ability to glow when they are apparently not illuminated by any visible source. Luminescent substances give off light when all other objects about the stage are invisible. For ghostly and novel effects this phenomenon is useful. There are two types of chemical pigments that have this property; one is phosphorescent and glows without any stimulus after it is once charged; the other is fluorescent and requires a constant stimulus in the form of invisible ultra violet (U. V.) light. The glow of both types of luminous pigments is so weak when other lights are on, that when they are used the stage should be as dark as possible. For the second type, a high-powered incandescent source must be used even if the throw is short (not over 12′).

An arc gives richer ultra violet light than the incandescent lamp, as well as greater intensity. High-powered light sources are necessary because the medium must filter out the visible light and pass only the U. V. The light absorbed turns into heat and the heat of the light source also affects the medium, so that it is well to immerse the U. V. medium in a water jacket. Glass tends to absorb U. V. rays so that a special quartz lens will increase the U. V. intensity. Luminescent chemicals can be had in several shades, which often glow with quite a different color from that which they appear to have under natural or visible light, in the form of paint, dye, and make-up. They are apt to be expensive, but a little goes a long way.

Beams of light play an important part in recent artistic photography and, more often than not, it is a difficult problem to eliminate them from the stage picture if the background of the setting is dark. Unfortunately, however, it is difficult to produce strong beams of light when they are wanted as part of the design, without resorting to very high-powered instruments of the searchlight type. The beam is seen only because of reflection from particles in the air so that either a great deal of dust or moisture must be present or some reflecting medium such as smoke or gauze must pick it up.

Gauze (often called scrim) has been mentioned previously, as a valuable medium for giving a hazy effect. It can be purchased in 30′ widths in several shades of blue, white, black or gray and in several types of mesh. It has no seams and it should completely cover the opening so that its edge is not seen. Generally, it should be stretched tightly, but draped gauze gives a soft rhythm of transparent folds, if they are desired.

When stretched tightly, a gauze may be lighted by strips, placed on the floor and suspended above. The strips should cast a sheet of light over the surface, preferably from the front, so that the illumination is even, or definitely graded as desired. A gauze lighted in this way gives a hazy appearance to any object lighted behind it. If the light is taken off the gauze, it practically disappears and objects are seen through it as if it were not there. It is impossible to project through a gauze to an object because the beam of light will make a distracting pattern where it strikes the surface of the gauze. By using several layers of gauze and appliquéd forms of trees or other objects it is possible to create a sense of great depth in a very shallow space. It is well to note, however, that more than one thickness of gauze gives a definite water mark effect, and an appearance of motion, to anyone in the audience who moves his head.

A translucent curtain can replace the backdrop when a Linnebach lantern or effect machine is used from behind. It is difficult to obtain cloth in widths greater than 9' in this country, so that there will have to be several seams showing if the curtain is at all large. To make ordinary muslin or canvas translucent, it can be treated with shellac and glycerin or simply wet down if it is to be used only for a short time. The position of any light source placed behind the curtain must be concealed. A vivid sky and cloud effect can be obtained by painting opaque clouds on the curtain, particularly over the seams, and lighting the curtain from both the front and rear, perhaps in the colors of sunset. The clouds can be made to take on the color of the light from the front and the translucent area will show the stronger colors directed on the curtain from the rear.

APPENDIX

Schedule of spread and intensity for spotlights

Plano-convex:

Watts	Lens	Spot	°	Med.	°	Flood	°
				Maximum Candle Power Beam Spread			
250	5 x 9	10,000	15	2,000	30	1,000	60
400	5 x 9	20,000	15	3,500	30	1,700	60
500	6 x 10	48,000	10	5,000	25	2,500	45
1000	6 x 10	90,000	10	11,000	25	4,500	45
1500	8 x 12	135,000	10	40,000	30	10,000	50
2000	8 x 12	195,000	10	55,000	30	14,000	50

Fresnel:

Candle Power at various beam spreads

100 Watt	3 x 2½	4,000	15	2,500	25	1,000	40
250 Watt	6 x 3½	25,000	15	6,500	40	3,000	60
500 Watt	6 x 3½	60,000	15	14,000	40	7,200	60
750 Watt	6 x 3½	72,000	15	22,000	40	8,000	60
1000 Watt	8 x 4¾	100,000	15	55,000	25	25,000	45
1500 Watt	8 x 4¾	160,000	15	80,000	25	38,000	45
2000 Watt	10 x 5¾	220,000	15	100,000	25	45,000	45
5000 Watt	14 x 8	600,000	15	300,000	25	100,000	45

Ellipsoidal:

Candle Power and beam spread

			Center	edge	degree-spread
500	2— 4½ x 6½	P.C.	11,400	5,000	48
500	2— 6 x 9	P.C.	23,000	3,000	35
750	2— 6 x 9	P.C.	28,000	4,000	35
500	2— 6 x 8	Step	18,000	2,000	40
750	2— 6 x 8	Step	23,000	3,000	40
500	2— 6 x 11	Step	30,000	3,500	30
750	2— 6 x 11	Step	44,000	5,000	30
500	1— 6 x 6	Step	35,000	5,000	25
750	1— 6 x 6	Step	55,000	6,000	25
750	1— 8 x 10	P.C.	85,000	10,000	18
750	1— 8 x 9	Step	90,000	15,000	20
1000	1— 8 x 9	Step	90,000	15,000	23
2000	1— 8 x 9	Step	160,000	30,000	23
3000	1—12 x 20	Step	650,000	400,000	12
5000	1—12 x 20	Step	850,000	550,000	12